The Future of Agriculture: Winners and Losers in a Post-Global Warming World

Copyright Page

TITLE: The Future of Agriculture: Winners and Losers in a Post-Global Warming World

1ST Edition

Copyright @ 2023

ISBN: 9798223339298

Table of Contents

The Future of Agriculture: Winners and Losers in a Post-Global Warming World

BY Roberto Miguel Rodriguez

Chapter 1: Agricultural Lands Post-Global Warming: Winners and Losers

In this book, we will explore the various aspects of post-global warming agricultural lands. As the effects of climate change continue to shape our world, it is crucial for policymakers, educators, journalists, and the public to understand the winners and losers in agriculture and devise sustainable solutions for the future.

One of the key topics to consider is the impact of global warming on agricultural lands. We will analyze which regions are likely to thrive and which may face challenges due to changing climate patterns. By understanding these dynamics, policymakers and legislators can make informed decisions about resource allocation and support for farmers in different regions.

To ensure the longevity and productivity of post-global warming agricultural lands, sustainable farming methods must be adopted. We will delve into various strategies, such as organic farming, regenerative agriculture, and agroecology, that promote soil health, biodiversity, and efficient resource management. These methods not only enhance resilience but also reduce the environmental footprint of agriculture.

Crop diversification is another crucial aspect of adapting to post-global warming conditions. We will explore the benefits of cultivating a wider range of crops to mitigate risks associated with changing climate patterns. By diversifying crop varieties, farmers can ensure a more stable income and reduce the vulnerability of their agricultural systems.

Resilient plant varieties play a vital role in thriving in post-global warming agricultural lands. We will discuss the importance of investing in research and development of climate-resistant crop varieties that can withstand extreme weather events and changing environmental conditions. This will enable farmers to continue producing high-quality crops even in challenging circumstances.

Water management techniques for irrigation in post-global warming agricultural lands are essential to optimize water use and minimize waste. We will explore innovative practices such as precision irrigation, drip irrigation, and rainwater harvesting, which can help farmers adapt to water scarcity and ensure sustainable agricultural production.

Maintaining soil fertility is crucial for long-term agricultural success. We will discuss soil restoration methods such as cover cropping, crop rotation, and organic matter management, which can enhance soil health, nutrient retention, and carbon sequestration. These practices not only contribute to sustainable agriculture but also mitigate climate change by reducing greenhouse gas emissions.

Pest and disease control strategies are vital for protecting crops in post-global warming agricultural lands. We will explore integrated pest management techniques, biological control methods, and the use of resistant crop varieties to minimize the use of chemical pesticides and promote ecological balance.

Agroforestry practices can play a significant role in climate adaptation for agriculture. We will discuss the benefits of integrating trees and shrubs into agricultural landscapes, such as improved soil health, enhanced biodiversity, and increased resilience to extreme weather events. Agroforestry systems also provide additional income streams through the production of timber, fruits, or medicinal plants.

Livestock management techniques need to be adapted to ensure sustainable farming in post-global warming agricultural lands. We will explore strategies such as rotational grazing, improved feed management, and waste management to minimize environmental impacts and enhance animal welfare.

Agricultural policy reforms are essential for supporting farmers in post-global warming conditions. We will discuss the importance of providing incentives for sustainable practices, promoting access to finance and insurance, and fostering innovation and knowledge transfer. These policy reforms can help farmers adapt to changing conditions and thrive in the face of climate change.

Finally, we will explore climate-smart agricultural technologies that can optimize productivity in post-global warming lands. We will discuss the potential of precision agriculture, remote sensing, and data analytics to monitor and manage agricultural systems efficiently. These technologies can contribute to increased efficiency, reduced resource use, and improved decision-making for farmers.

By addressing these topics, this book aims to provide a comprehensive understanding of the challenges and opportunities in post-global warming agricultural lands. It is our hope that policymakers, diplomats, legislators, educators, journalists, and the public can use this knowledge to shape policies, practices, and public discourse towards a more sustainable and resilient future for agriculture.

Understanding the Impact of Global Warming on Agriculture

Chapter X: Understanding the Impact of Global Warming on Agriculture

Introduction:

Global warming is one of the biggest challenges our planet is facing. Its impact reaches far and wide, affecting various sectors, including agriculture. In this subchapter, we will explore the profound implications of global warming on agriculture and discuss strategies and techniques to adapt and thrive in a post-global warming world.

1. Agricultural Lands Post-Global Warming: Winners and Losers

Global warming will reshape agricultural landscapes, leading to winners and losers. Some regions may experience increased agricultural productivity, while others may face challenges due to changing climate patterns. We will examine the regions that are likely to benefit and those that will struggle and discuss potential solutions to mitigate the negative impacts.

2. Sustainable Farming Methods for Post-Global Warming Agricultural Lands

To ensure the long-term viability of agriculture in a post-global warming world, it is crucial to adopt sustainable farming practices. We will explore innovative techniques such as organic farming, agroecology, and precision agriculture that can enhance productivity while minimizing environmental degradation.

3. Crop Diversification Strategies for Adapting to Post-Global Warming Conditions

Global warming will alter the suitability of certain crops in different regions. Crop diversification is a key strategy to mitigate risks associated with climate change. We will discuss the importance of diversifying crops and provide guidance on selecting suitable crop varieties for specific climatic conditions.

4. Resilient Plant Varieties for Thriving in Post-Global Warming Agricultural Lands

Developing resilient plant varieties that can withstand the challenges posed by global warming is crucial. We will delve into the importance of plant breeding and genetic engineering techniques in developing climate-resilient crops that can thrive in extreme weather conditions.

5. Water Management Techniques for Irrigation in Post-Global Warming Agricultural Lands

Water scarcity will become a pressing issue in many regions due to global warming. We will discuss innovative water management techniques such as drip irrigation, rainwater harvesting, and efficient water use practices that can help farmers adapt to water scarcity and maintain agricultural productivity.

6. Soil Restoration Methods for Maintaining Fertility in Post-Global Warming Agricultural Lands

Global warming can lead to soil degradation and loss of fertility. We will explore soil restoration techniques such as cover cropping, crop rotation, and organic amendments that can help replenish nutrients, improve soil structure, and enhance its capacity to retain water.

7. Pest and Disease Control Strategies for Crops in Post-Global Warming Agricultural Lands

Changing climate patterns will exacerbate pest and disease problems in agriculture. We will discuss integrated pest management approaches, biocontrol methods, and the use of resistant crop varieties to mitigate the impact of pests and diseases on crops.

8. Agroforestry Practices for Climate Adaptation in Post-Global Warming Agricultural Lands

Agroforestry offers a promising solution for climate adaptation in agriculture. We will explore the benefits of integrating trees with crops and livestock, such as enhancing soil fertility, improving water retention, and providing shade and microclimatic regulation.

9. Livestock Management Techniques for Sustainable Farming in Post-Global Warming Agricultural Lands

Global warming will also impact livestock production. We will discuss sustainable livestock management techniques, including efficient feeding practices, improved breeding strategies, and alternative energy sources, to reduce greenhouse gas emissions and enhance the resilience of livestock systems.

10. Agricultural Policy Reforms for Supporting Farmers in Post-Global Warming Conditions

To ensure a smooth transition to a post-global warming agricultural system, policymakers need to implement supportive agricultural policies. We will explore policy reforms that can incentivize sustainable farming practices, provide financial support to farmers, and promote climate-smart agriculture.

11. Climate-Smart Agricultural Technologies for Optimizing Productivity in Post-Global Warming Lands

Advancements in technology can play a crucial role in adapting agriculture to the challenges posed by global warming. We will discuss climate-smart technologies such as precision agriculture, remote sensing, and digital farming tools that can optimize productivity, reduce resource use, and enhance resilience in a post-global warming world.

Conclusion:

Understanding the impact of global warming on agriculture is essential for policymakers, educators, journalists, and the public. By implementing sustainable farming methods, diversifying crops, developing resilient plant varieties, and adopting innovative water and soil management techniques, we can build a resilient agricultural system that can thrive in a post-global warming world. It is imperative that we act now to ensure the future of agriculture for generations to come.

Identifying Regions Benefiting from Global Warming

Subchapter: Identifying Regions Benefiting from Global Warming

Introduction:

In this subchapter, we will explore the potential winners and losers in a post-global warming world, specifically focusing on identifying regions that could benefit from the changing climate. As policymakers, diplomats, legislators, educators, journalists, and the public, it is crucial to understand the implications of global warming on agricultural lands and its subsequent effects on sustainable farming, crop diversification, plant varieties, water management, soil restoration, pest control, agroforestry, livestock management, agricultural policy reforms, and climate-smart technologies.

1. Agricultural Lands Post-Global Warming: Winners and Losers:

In this section, we will analyze different regions around the world and determine which ones may experience positive outcomes due to global warming. We will consider factors such as temperature changes, precipitation patterns, and soil conditions to identify regions that could potentially see increased agricultural productivity and profitability.

2. Sustainable Farming Methods for Post-Global Warming Agricultural Lands:

To ensure long-term viability and environmental sustainability, this section will explore innovative and eco-friendly farming techniques suitable for regions benefiting from global warming. We will discuss practices such as organic farming, precision agriculture, and regenerative agriculture that can optimize productivity while minimizing negative impacts on the environment.

3. Crop Diversification Strategies for Adapting to Post-Global Warming Conditions:

As climate conditions change, farmers will need to adapt their crop choices. This section will provide insights into crop diversification strategies that can help farmers mitigate risks and take advantage of new opportunities presented by global warming-induced changes in temperature, rainfall, and growing seasons.

4. Resilient Plant Varieties for Thriving in Post-Global Warming Agricultural Lands:

To ensure successful crop production in a changing climate, farmers will need access to resilient plant varieties that can withstand higher temperatures, water stress, and new pest and disease pressures. This section will discuss breeding programs, genetic engineering, and other approaches to develop climate-adaptive plant varieties.

5. Water Management Techniques for Irrigation in Post-Global Warming Agricultural Lands:

With changing precipitation patterns, efficient water management becomes crucial. This section will explore innovative irrigation techniques such as drip irrigation, precision irrigation, and rainwater harvesting to ensure optimal water use and minimize water stress on crops.

6. Soil Restoration Methods for Maintaining Fertility in Post-Global Warming Agricultural Lands:

Global warming can pose challenges to soil fertility and health. This section will provide insights into soil restoration techniques like cover cropping, crop rotation, and organic amendments that can enhance soil structure, nutrient content, and microbial activity in post-global warming agricultural lands.

7. Pest and Disease Control Strategies for Crops in Post-Global Warming Agricultural Lands:

As the climate changes, new pests and diseases may emerge, posing threats to crop productivity. This section will discuss integrated pest management practices, biocontrol methods, and early warning systems to mitigate the impact of pests and diseases in a changing climate.

8. Agroforestry Practices for Climate Adaptation in Post-Global Warming Agricultural Lands:

Agroforestry systems can provide multiple benefits such as carbon sequestration, soil conservation, and biodiversity enhancement. This section will explore how integrating trees into farming systems can help farmers adapt to climate change while improving overall resilience and sustainability.

9. Livestock Management Techniques for Sustainable Farming in Post-Global Warming Agricultural Lands:

This section will focus on livestock management practices that promote animal welfare, reduce greenhouse gas emissions, and improve resource efficiency. We will discuss strategies such as rotational grazing, feed optimization, and waste management to ensure sustainable livestock farming in a post-global warming world.

10. Agricultural Policy Reforms for Supporting Farmers in Post-Global Warming Conditions:

To facilitate the transition to a post-global warming agricultural landscape, policymakers need to implement supportive policies and incentives. This section will highlight key policy reforms that can help farmers adapt, innovate, and thrive in a changing climate while ensuring food security and rural development.

11. Climate-Smart Agricultural Technologies for Optimizing Productivity in Post-Global Warming Lands:

The final section will delve into cutting-edge technologies that can enhance productivity, resource efficiency, and climate resilience in post-global warming agricultural lands. We will explore technologies such as precision farming, remote sensing, data analytics, and smart irrigation systems that can revolutionize farming practices in the future.

Conclusion:

By identifying regions that may benefit from global warming, we can develop targeted strategies and policies to support sustainable agriculture in a changing climate. Through the adoption of innovative practices, resilient plant varieties, efficient water and soil management, and climate-smart technologies, farmers can adapt to new conditions and ensure a prosperous future for agriculture in a post-global warming world.

Examining Regions Facing Challenges in a Post-Global Warming World

In a rapidly changing world impacted by global warming, it is crucial to examine the regions that will face significant challenges in adapting to these new conditions. From agricultural lands to sustainable farming methods, this subchapter delves into the winners and losers in a post-global warming world and provides insights for policymakers, educators, journalists, and the public.

Agricultural Lands Post-Global Warming: Winners and Losers

This section explores the regions that will be winners and losers in the post-global warming era. It analyzes the potential impacts of rising temperatures, changing precipitation patterns, and extreme weather events on crop production and food security. By understanding the vulnerabilities and strengths of different regions, policymakers can devise targeted strategies to mitigate the negative impacts and harness potential opportunities.

Sustainable Farming Methods for Post-Global Warming Agricultural Lands

To ensure the long-term viability of agriculture in a post-global warming world, sustainable farming practices are essential. This section highlights innovative techniques such as organic farming, agroecology, and permaculture that promote soil health, reduce greenhouse gas emissions, and enhance biodiversity. By implementing these methods, farmers can adapt to changing conditions while protecting the environment.

Crop Diversification Strategies for Adapting to Post-Global Warming Conditions

In a warmer world, certain crops may struggle to thrive, while others may benefit from the changing climate. This section explores the importance of diversifying crop varieties to reduce vulnerability and increase resilience. By embracing a wider range of crops that are better suited to changing conditions, farmers can adapt to the post-global warming landscape and ensure food security.

Resilient Plant Varieties for Thriving in Post-Global Warming Agricultural Lands

As temperatures rise and weather patterns become unpredictable, it is crucial to develop and promote resilient plant varieties. This section discusses the importance of breeding and cultivating crops that can withstand heat stress, drought, and pests. By investing in research and development, farmers can access crops that are better adapted to the challenges of a post-global warming world.

Water Management Techniques for Irrigation in Post-Global Warming Agricultural Lands

Water scarcity is a growing concern in many regions, exacerbated by global warming. This section explores innovative water management techniques such as drip irrigation, rainwater harvesting, and precision agriculture. By maximizing water efficiency and reducing waste, farmers can adapt to changing precipitation patterns while minimizing their environmental impact.

Soil Restoration Methods for Maintaining Fertility in Post-Global Warming Agricultural Lands

Healthy soils are the foundation of sustainable agriculture. This section discusses soil restoration methods, including cover cropping, crop rotation, and composting, to maintain soil fertility and enhance resilience. By adopting these practices, farmers can mitigate the effects of global warming on soil health and ensure the long-term productivity of their lands.

Pest and Disease Control Strategies for Crops in Post-Global Warming Agricultural Lands

As the climate changes, pests and diseases may become more prevalent and challenging to control. This section explores integrated pest management techniques, biological control, and the use of resistant crop varieties. By implementing effective pest and disease control strategies, farmers can safeguard their crops and minimize yield losses in a post-global warming world.

Agroforestry Practices for Climate Adaptation in Post-Global Warming Agricultural Lands

Agroforestry offers a promising solution for adapting to a changing climate. This section explores the integration of trees with agricultural crops, providing multiple benefits such as shade, windbreaks, and soil conservation. By implementing agroforestry practices, farmers can enhance climate resilience, diversify their income streams, and improve ecosystem services.

Livestock Management Techniques for Sustainable Farming in Post-Global Warming Agricultural Lands

Livestock farming is also vulnerable to the impacts of global warming. This section discusses sustainable livestock management techniques such as rotational grazing, improved feed efficiency, and waste management. By adopting these practices, farmers can reduce greenhouse gas emissions, enhance animal welfare, and ensure the long-term viability of their livestock operations.

Agricultural Policy Reforms for Supporting Farmers in Post-Global Warming Conditions

To navigate the challenges of a post-global warming world, policymakers must enact agricultural policy reforms that support farmers. This section examines the importance of investment in research and development, access to credit and insurance, and the creation of market incentives for sustainable practices. By implementing appropriate policies, governments can empower farmers to adapt and thrive in changing conditions.

Climate-Smart Agricultural Technologies for Optimizing Productivity in Post-Global Warming Lands

Technological innovation plays a crucial role in sustainable agriculture. This section explores climate-smart agricultural technologies such as precision farming, remote sensing, and digital tools for decision-making. By harnessing these technologies, farmers can optimize productivity, reduce resource use, and minimize environmental impacts in a post-global warming world.

In conclusion, this subchapter provides a comprehensive examination of the challenges and opportunities faced by regions in a post-global warming world. By understanding the winners and losers, embracing sustainable farming methods, diversifying crops, promoting resilient plant varieties, adopting water and soil management techniques, implementing pest and disease control strategies, integrating agroforestry practices, improving livestock management, enacting agricultural policy reforms, and leveraging climate-smart technologies, we can navigate the complexities of a changing climate and ensure a prosperous future for agriculture.

Assessing the Economic and Social Implications of Climate Change on Agriculture

Introduction:

Climate change is a pressing issue that has significant economic and social implications for agriculture. As global temperatures rise and extreme weather events become more frequent, agricultural lands face various challenges. This subchapter aims to explore the potential consequences of climate change on agriculture, as well as propose strategies to mitigate its impact and adapt to post-global warming conditions. It is essential for policymakers, diplomats, legislators, educators, journalists, and the public to understand these implications and work towards sustainable solutions.

Economic Implications:

The economic implications of climate change on agriculture are far-reaching. Changes in temperature and precipitation patterns can lead to reduced crop yields, increased production costs, and decreased profitability for farmers. This, in turn, can lead to food insecurity, rising food prices, and increased poverty levels. Therefore, it is crucial to develop sustainable farming methods, diversify crops, and promote resilient plant varieties to ensure agricultural productivity and economic stability.

Social Implications:

Climate change also has significant social implications for agriculture. Changes in weather patterns can disrupt traditional farming practices, leading to displacement and migration of farmers and agricultural communities. Moreover, the loss of agricultural livelihoods can result in social unrest and political instability. To address these challenges, policymakers must focus on implementing effective agricultural policy reforms that support farmers and ensure social equity.

Mitigation and Adaptation Strategies:

To mitigate and adapt to the impact of climate change on agriculture, several strategies can be implemented. Sustainable farming methods such as organic farming and precision agriculture can reduce greenhouse gas emissions and minimize the use of chemical inputs. Crop diversification strategies can enhance resilience to changing climatic conditions, while the development and adoption of resilient plant varieties can ensure crop survival and productivity. Water management techniques, such as drip irrigation and rainwater harvesting, can optimize water use efficiency in agriculture. Soil restoration methods, including cover cropping and conservation tillage, can maintain soil fertility and reduce erosion. Pest and disease control strategies, such as integrated pest management, can minimize crop losses. Agroforestry practices can provide climate adaptation benefits, such as carbon sequestration and improved microclimate. Sustainable livestock management techniques, such as rotational grazing, can reduce the environmental impact of animal agriculture. Additionally, agricultural policy reforms should focus on supporting farmers in adapting to post-global warming conditions through financial incentives, research and development, and capacity-building programs. Lastly, the adoption of climate-smart agricultural technologies, including precision farming tools and remote sensing technologies, can optimize productivity in post-global warming agricultural lands.

Conclusion:

Assessing the economic and social implications of climate change on agriculture is crucial for policymakers, diplomats, legislators, educators, journalists, and the public. By understanding these implications and implementing sustainable farming methods, diversifying crops, promoting resilient plant varieties, managing water resources, restoring soil fertility, controlling pests and diseases, adopting agroforestry practices, managing livestock sustainably, enacting agricultural policy reforms, and adopting climate-smart technologies, society can work towards a future where agriculture can thrive in a post-global warming world. It is essential to prioritize these strategies to ensure the resilience and sustainability of agricultural lands in the face of climate change.

Chapter 2: Sustainable Farming Methods for Post-Global Warming Agricultural Lands

Introduction to Sustainable Farming

In a rapidly changing world, the future of agriculture is at a critical juncture. With the looming threat of global warming, it is imperative that we adapt our farming practices to ensure the resilience and sustainability of our agricultural lands. This subchapter, titled "Introduction to Sustainable Farming," aims to provide an overview of the key principles and strategies necessary for successful farming in a post-global warming world.

As politicians, diplomats, legislators, educators, journalists, and the public, it is our collective duty to understand the challenges that lie ahead and work towards solutions that promote sustainable agriculture. This subchapter will delve into various aspects of sustainable farming, addressing the specific niches of agricultural lands post-global warming, crop diversification strategies, resilient plant varieties, water management techniques, soil restoration methods, pest and disease control strategies, agroforestry practices, livestock management techniques, agricultural policy reforms, and climate-smart agricultural technologies.

With global warming altering climatic conditions, agricultural lands will experience winners and losers. Some regions may become more favorable for farming, while others may face significant challenges. By understanding these dynamics, we can make informed decisions about which crops to grow and where to allocate resources.

Crop diversification will be crucial for adapting to post-global warming conditions. By growing a variety of crops, farmers can reduce the risk of crop failure and maintain productivity in the face of changing environmental conditions.

To ensure the survival of our crops, it is essential to cultivate resilient plant varieties that can thrive in the new climatic realities. This includes using techniques such as genetic modification and selective breeding to develop plants with increased tolerance to heat, drought, and pests.

Water management techniques will play a vital role in sustainable farming. With changing rainfall patterns and increased water scarcity, farmers must adopt efficient irrigation methods, such as drip irrigation and precision agriculture, to optimize water usage.

Maintaining soil fertility is another critical consideration in post-global warming agricultural lands. Soil restoration methods, such as cover cropping, crop rotation, and organic farming practices, can enhance soil health and productivity.

Pest and disease control strategies must also be adapted to the changing climate. Integrated pest management, crop rotation, and biological controls can help minimize the impact of pests and diseases without relying heavily on chemical interventions.

Agroforestry, the practice of integrating trees with crops and livestock, offers multiple benefits for climate adaptation. Trees provide shade, windbreaks, and additional sources of income, while also sequestering carbon and improving soil health.

Livestock management techniques should focus on sustainable practices that minimize environmental impact. This includes promoting rotational grazing, reducing antibiotic use, and adopting feed strategies that lower methane emissions.

Agricultural policy reforms are essential for supporting farmers in post-global warming conditions. These policies should incentivize sustainable farming practices, provide financial support for adaptation measures, and promote knowledge sharing among farmers.

Lastly, the integration of climate-smart agricultural technologies can optimize productivity in post-global warming lands. This includes the use of precision farming tools, remote sensing technologies, and data analytics to make informed decisions and maximize resource efficiency.

In conclusion, sustainable farming is the key to ensuring food security and environmental resilience in a post-global warming world. By adopting appropriate strategies and technologies, we can mitigate the challenges ahead and build a more sustainable future for agriculture. It is essential that policymakers, educators, journalists, and the public come together to support and promote sustainable farming practices for the benefit of present and future generations.

Organic Farming Techniques for Climate Adaptation

In a world grappling with the effects of global warming, it is imperative that we explore sustainable farming methods that can help us adapt to the changing climate. Organic farming techniques offer a promising solution for agricultural lands in the post-global warming era. This subchapter focuses on the various organic farming techniques that can be employed to ensure the resilience of our agricultural systems.

One key strategy for adapting to post-global warming conditions is sustainable crop diversification. By cultivating a diverse range of crops, farmers can reduce their vulnerability to climate change impacts. Different crops have varying tolerances to temperature, precipitation, and pests. By diversifying their crop portfolio, farmers can increase the chances of having a successful harvest despite unpredictable weather patterns.

Another crucial aspect of climate adaptation is the use of resilient plant varieties. In a post-global warming world, farmers need to select and cultivate plant varieties that are better suited to withstand extreme weather events, such as droughts or floods. These resilient varieties have been bred or naturally selected for their ability to thrive under challenging conditions, ensuring a more stable food supply.

Water management techniques also play a vital role in adapting to post-global warming conditions. With changing rainfall patterns, farmers need to optimize their irrigation practices to ensure efficient water use. This may involve the adoption of drip irrigation systems, rainwater harvesting, or the use of moisture sensors to determine the precise water requirements of crops.

Maintaining soil fertility is another critical challenge in a post-global warming agricultural landscape. Organic farming techniques, such as the use of compost, cover crops, and crop rotation, can help restore and enhance soil health. Healthy soils not only improve crop productivity but also contribute to carbon sequestration, mitigating climate change.

Pest and disease control strategies are also essential in a changing climate. Organic farming techniques emphasize the use of biological control methods, such as beneficial insects or resistant plant varieties, to minimize the use of chemical pesticides. This approach not only protects the environment but also ensures the long-term sustainability of our agricultural systems.

Agroforestry practices offer another climate-smart strategy for adaptation. By integrating trees into agricultural landscapes, farmers can enhance biodiversity, improve soil quality, and provide shade and windbreaks for crops. Agroforestry systems also sequester carbon, offering a nature-based solution to climate change mitigation.

Livestock management techniques should also be addressed in post-global warming agricultural lands. Sustainable grazing practices, such as rotational grazing or silvopasture, can minimize the environmental impact of livestock production while promoting healthier ecosystems.

To support farmers in these changing conditions, agricultural policy reforms are necessary. Governments and institutions should prioritize policies that incentivize and support organic farming practices, provide access to resources and knowledge, and ensure fair market opportunities for organic produce.

Lastly, the integration of climate-smart agricultural technologies can optimize productivity in post-global warming lands. Technologies such as precision farming, remote sensing, and data analytics can help farmers make informed decisions and manage their resources more efficiently.

In conclusion, organic farming techniques offer a pathway towards climate adaptation in a post-global warming world. By employing sustainable farming methods, diversifying crops, using resilient plant varieties, managing water and soil effectively, controlling pests and diseases organically, practicing agroforestry, managing livestock sustainably, implementing agricultural policy reforms, and embracing climate-smart technologies, we can ensure the resilience and sustainability of our agricultural systems in the face of a changing climate. Policymakers, educators, journalists, and the public must come together to promote and support these organic farming techniques for a future where agriculture thrives despite the challenges posed by global warming.

Regenerative Agriculture Practices for Soil Health

In the face of a post-global warming world, it is imperative that we prioritize the health of our agricultural lands. One of the key factors in ensuring the long-term sustainability of our food production systems is soil health. Regenerative agriculture practices offer a solution to not only maintain but also improve the fertility and resilience of our soils.

Regenerative agriculture focuses on rebuilding soil organic matter, restoring biodiversity, and enhancing ecosystem services. By adopting these practices, we can mitigate the negative effects of climate change on our agricultural lands while also increasing productivity and profitability for farmers.

One of the key strategies for regenerative agriculture is the use of cover crops. By planting a diverse range of cover crops such as legumes, grasses, and brassicas, farmers can protect the soil from erosion, improve water infiltration, and increase the availability of nutrients. These cover crops also contribute to the sequestration of carbon, reducing greenhouse gas emissions and mitigating the effects of climate change.

Another important aspect of regenerative agriculture is crop diversification. By growing a variety of crops, farmers can reduce the risk of crop failure due to extreme weather events and pest outbreaks. Crop rotation, intercropping, and agroforestry practices can also help improve soil structure, nutrient cycling, and pest control.

Water management techniques are crucial for irrigation in post-global warming agricultural lands. Efficient irrigation systems such as drip irrigation and precision irrigation can minimize water wastage and improve water-use efficiency. Additionally, the adoption of water-conserving practices like mulching and conservation tillage can help retain soil moisture and reduce the need for irrigation.

Soil restoration methods, such as the use of organic amendments and compost, can enhance soil fertility and structure. These practices promote the growth of beneficial soil microorganisms, improve nutrient availability, and increase water-holding capacity. By maintaining healthy soils, farmers can ensure the long-term productivity of their lands.

Pest and disease control strategies in post-global warming agricultural lands must prioritize integrated pest management (IPM) approaches. IPM combines biological, cultural, and chemical control methods to minimize the use of pesticides and prevent pest resistance. By promoting natural predators, crop rotation, and resistant plant varieties, farmers can effectively manage pests and diseases while minimizing the negative environmental impacts.

Agroforestry practices, such as the integration of trees and crops, offer multiple benefits in a post-global warming world. Trees provide shade, windbreaks, and habitat for beneficial insects, while also sequestering carbon and improving soil fertility. Agroforestry systems can enhance biodiversity, reduce soil erosion, and provide additional income streams for farmers through the production of timber, fruits, and nuts.

Livestock management techniques should prioritize sustainable practices such as rotational grazing, pasture management, and the use of organic feed. These practices can improve soil health, reduce methane emissions, and enhance animal welfare. By adopting regenerative livestock management, farmers can contribute to climate change mitigation while also ensuring the long-term viability of their farming operations.

To support farmers in a post-global warming world, agricultural policy reforms are necessary. Policies that incentivize the adoption of regenerative agriculture practices, provide financial support for sustainable farming methods, and promote research and education are essential. By creating a supportive policy environment, we can empower farmers to transition to climate-smart agricultural practices and ensure the resilience of our agricultural lands.

In conclusion, regenerative agriculture practices offer a promising solution for maintaining soil health in a post-global warming world. By prioritizing strategies such as cover cropping, crop diversification, water management, soil restoration, pest control, agroforestry, and sustainable livestock management, we can ensure the long-term sustainability and productivity of our agricultural lands. It is crucial for politicians, diplomats, legislators, educators, journalists, and the public to recognize the importance of regenerative agriculture and support policies and practices that promote its adoption.

Precision Farming Technologies for Resource Optimization

In the face of a post-global warming world, the future of agriculture depends on the adoption of innovative technologies that optimize resources and mitigate the impact of climate change. Precision farming technologies offer a promising solution for sustainable and efficient agricultural practices in this challenging era. This subchapter will explore the various precision farming technologies and their potential to optimize resources in post-global warming agricultural lands.

Precision farming involves the use of advanced technologies such as GPS, remote sensing, and data analytics to monitor and manage agricultural practices with precision. These technologies enable farmers to make informed decisions and optimize the use of resources like water, soil, and fertilizers, resulting in higher yields and reduced environmental impact.

One key area where precision farming technologies can be applied is water management. With the increasing scarcity of water resources, it is crucial to employ irrigation techniques that are both efficient and sustainable. Precision farming technologies, such as soil moisture sensors and automated irrigation systems, can help farmers optimize water usage by providing real-time data on soil moisture levels and crop water requirements. This ensures that water is applied only when and where it is needed, reducing water wastage and improving overall water-use efficiency.

Another important aspect of resource optimization in post-global warming agricultural lands is soil restoration. Precision farming technologies can aid in maintaining soil fertility by providing accurate information about soil composition and nutrient levels. This allows farmers to apply fertilizers and soil amendments precisely, avoiding overuse or underuse. Additionally, precision technologies can help identify areas of the field that are prone to erosion or nutrient depletion, enabling targeted interventions to prevent further degradation.

Precision farming technologies also play a crucial role in pest and disease control. By utilizing sensors and imaging technologies, farmers can detect and monitor pest infestations or disease outbreaks at an early stage. This allows for timely intervention, reducing the reliance on chemical pesticides and minimizing the environmental impact.

Furthermore, precision farming technologies can facilitate the adoption of climate-smart agricultural practices, such as crop diversification and agroforestry. These practices contribute to the resilience of agricultural systems by enhancing biodiversity, conserving soil moisture, and reducing greenhouse gas emissions. Precision technologies provide farmers with the necessary information to implement these practices effectively and optimize their benefits.

In conclusion, precision farming technologies offer immense potential for optimizing resources in post-global warming agricultural lands. By enabling precise control over irrigation, soil fertility, pest control, and climate-smart practices, these technologies can help farmers adapt to the challenges of a changing climate while ensuring sustainable and productive agricultural systems. Policymakers, educators, journalists, and the public should support the widespread adoption of precision farming technologies and advocate for agricultural policy reforms that incentivize their implementation. By embracing these technologies, we can secure a prosperous and resilient future for agriculture in a post-global warming world.

Chapter 3: Crop Diversification Strategies for Adapting to Post-Global Warming Conditions

Importance of Crop Diversification in a Changing Climate

In a rapidly changing climate, the importance of crop diversification cannot be overstated. As the world faces the challenges of global warming and its impact on agricultural lands, it is crucial to adopt strategies that will ensure food security and sustainability for future generations. Crop diversification offers a practical and effective solution to mitigate the risks associated with climate change and adapt to the new realities of post-global warming agricultural lands.

One of the key benefits of crop diversification is its ability to enhance resilience in the face of unpredictable weather patterns. By cultivating a variety of crops, farmers can spread their risks and reduce vulnerability to the adverse effects of climate change. Diverse crops can have different tolerances to temperature fluctuations, drought, or excessive rainfall, ensuring that at least some crops will thrive under changing conditions. This not only safeguards farmers' livelihoods but also ensures a stable food supply for local communities and beyond.

Furthermore, crop diversification promotes sustainable farming methods. Monoculture, which is the practice of growing a single crop over large areas, is highly susceptible to pests and diseases. By diversifying crops, farmers can break the cycle of pest and disease outbreaks, reducing the need for chemical inputs and promoting natural pest control mechanisms. This not only protects the environment but also reduces the economic burden on farmers.

Crop diversification also plays a crucial role in maintaining soil fertility and health in post-global warming agricultural lands. Different crops have varying nutrient requirements, which can help prevent soil depletion and erosion. Additionally, some crops, such as legumes, have the ability to fix nitrogen in the soil, reducing the need for synthetic fertilizers. This sustainable approach to soil management ensures the long-term viability of agricultural lands and preserves their productivity for future generations.

Moreover, crop diversification can contribute to climate change mitigation efforts. Certain crops, such as trees and perennial plants, have the ability to sequester carbon dioxide from the atmosphere, helping to reduce greenhouse gas emissions. By integrating agroforestry practices into farming systems, farmers can not only adapt to a changing climate but also contribute to the global effort to combat climate change.

In conclusion, crop diversification is a crucial strategy for adapting to the challenges of a changing climate in post-global warming agricultural lands. By spreading risks, promoting sustainable farming methods, maintaining soil fertility, and contributing to climate change mitigation, crop diversification offers a path towards resilience and sustainability. Policymakers, diplomats, legislators, educators, journalists, and the public must recognize the importance of crop diversification and support agricultural policy reforms that encourage farmers to adopt these strategies. Additionally, investment in climate-smart agricultural technologies and research on resilient plant varieties can further optimize productivity in a post-global warming world. Only by embracing crop diversification and sustainable farming practices can we ensure a prosperous and food-secure future for all.

Selecting Resilient Crop Varieties for Different Climate Zones

In a rapidly changing world affected by global warming, the agricultural sector faces numerous challenges. Farmers and policymakers must adapt to new climate conditions to ensure food security and sustainable farming practices. One crucial aspect of this adaptation is selecting resilient crop varieties suitable for different climate zones.

The selection of crop varieties that can thrive in specific climate zones is essential for maximizing productivity and minimizing potential losses. As politicians, diplomats, legislators, educators, journalists, and the public, understanding the importance of this process is crucial in supporting sustainable agriculture in a post-global warming world.

Different climate zones have unique environmental conditions, such as temperature, humidity, and rainfall patterns. Therefore, it is necessary to identify crop varieties that can withstand these specific conditions. Resilient crop varieties possess traits such as heat and drought tolerance, disease resistance, and adaptability to changing weather patterns.

To ensure the success of crop selection, collaboration between scientists, farmers, and agricultural experts is crucial. Research institutions can provide valuable information on the performance of different crop varieties under specific climate conditions. Farmers can contribute their local knowledge and experience to identify varieties that have historically performed well in their regions. By combining these efforts, policymakers can develop strategies to support the adoption of resilient crop varieties.

Additionally, education and awareness campaigns are essential to inform farmers about the benefits of selecting resilient crop varieties. Training programs and workshops can provide farmers with the necessary skills to identify, evaluate, and select suitable varieties for their specific climate zones. By investing in education and capacity-building, policymakers can empower farmers to make informed decisions that contribute to the long-term sustainability of their agricultural practices.

In conclusion, selecting resilient crop varieties for different climate zones is a crucial step in adapting to a post-global warming world. By supporting research, collaboration, and education, policymakers can promote sustainable farming practices and ensure food security in the face of a changing climate. It is imperative that politicians, diplomats, legislators, educators, journalists, and the public recognize the significance of this subchapter and actively engage in efforts to support resilient crop selection.

Rotational Cropping Systems for Pest and Disease Control

In the face of the challenges posed by global warming, agricultural lands must adapt to ensure food security and sustainable farming practices. One crucial aspect of this adaptation is the implementation of effective pest and disease control strategies. Rotational cropping systems have emerged as a promising solution for managing pests and diseases while maintaining the productivity of agricultural lands in a post-global warming world.

Rotational cropping is a practice that involves alternating different crops in a specific sequence over multiple growing seasons. This approach disrupts the life cycles of pests and diseases, reducing their population and minimizing the risk of outbreaks. By strategically planning crop rotations, farmers can control pests and diseases while promoting soil health and fertility.

One key advantage of rotational cropping systems is their ability to break the cycle of pests and diseases that often build up when the same crop is grown continuously in the same location. By rotating crops, farmers can prevent the buildup of pests and diseases that target specific plants. Additionally, some crops have natural pest-repellent properties, further enhancing the effectiveness of the rotation.

Crop diversification is an essential component of rotational cropping systems. By planting a diverse range of crops, farmers can decrease the risk of pest and disease outbreaks. Different crops attract different pests and diseases, meaning that a diverse crop rotation can disrupt their life cycles and reduce their overall impact.

Furthermore, resilient plant varieties that are adapted to post-global warming conditions should be prioritized in rotational cropping systems. These varieties are more resistant to pests and diseases, reducing the need for chemical interventions. By selecting and breeding such varieties, farmers can enhance the resilience of their crops and minimize the risk of yield losses.

To optimize the effectiveness of rotational cropping systems, integrated pest management (IPM) practices should be adopted. IPM combines various pest control methods, including biological control, cultural practices, and targeted chemical interventions, to minimize the use of pesticides while effectively managing pests and diseases.

In conclusion, rotational cropping systems offer a sustainable and effective approach to pest and disease control in a post-global warming world. By diversifying crops, integrating resilient plant varieties, and implementing integrated pest management practices, farmers can protect their crops while maintaining the long-term productivity and sustainability of agricultural lands. Policymakers, educators, journalists, and the public must recognize the importance of promoting and supporting these practices to ensure the future of agriculture in a changing climate.

Enhancing Crop Diversity through Intercropping Techniques

In the face of a post-global warming world, where agricultural lands are experiencing unprecedented challenges, it is imperative to explore innovative and sustainable farming methods. One such approach is intercropping, a technique that can enhance crop diversity and promote resilience in our agricultural systems.

Intercropping involves growing two or more crops simultaneously in the same field, allowing for the efficient use of resources and maximizing land productivity. By combining crops with different growth habits, nutrient requirements, and pest resistance, farmers can minimize the risk of crop failure and improve overall yields.

This subchapter aims to shed light on the importance of intercropping techniques in post-global warming agricultural lands. It delves into the potential benefits and challenges associated with this practice, and highlights how it can contribute to the sustainability and resilience of our food production systems.

Intercropping not only diversifies crop production but also plays a crucial role in maintaining soil fertility. By planting crops with varying root depths and nutrient requirements, intercropping helps prevent soil degradation and reduces the need for chemical fertilizers. This practice can mitigate the negative impacts of global warming on soil health and fertility, thus ensuring the long-term productivity of agricultural lands.

Furthermore, intercropping can act as a natural pest and disease control strategy. By disrupting the monoculture environment, intercropping creates a less favorable habitat for pests and diseases, reducing the reliance on chemical pesticides. This not only protects the environment but also safeguards human health and promotes the production of healthier, pesticide-free crops.

Intercropping also presents an opportunity for climate adaptation through agroforestry practices. By integrating trees with crops, farmers can create microclimates that provide shade, reduce evaporation, and prevent soil erosion. Additionally, the trees act as carbon sinks, mitigating the effects of greenhouse gas emissions and contributing to climate change mitigation efforts.

To fully realize the potential of intercropping, policymakers and agricultural stakeholders must recognize its significance and provide necessary support to farmers. This can include financial incentives, technical assistance, and research and development initiatives. By incorporating intercropping techniques into agricultural policies and programs, governments can help farmers adapt to post-global warming conditions and ensure a sustainable and resilient future for our food systems.

In conclusion, enhancing crop diversity through intercropping techniques is an essential strategy for adapting to the challenges posed by a post-global warming world. By harnessing the benefits of intercropping, we can promote sustainable farming practices, maintain soil fertility, reduce pest and disease risks, and contribute to climate change mitigation efforts. Policymakers, educators, journalists, and the public must join forces to support and promote intercropping as a key component of our agricultural future.

Chapter 4: Resilient Plant Varieties for Thriving in Post-Global Warming Agricultural Lands

Breeding Climate-Resilient Crop Varieties

In a rapidly changing world, where the consequences of global warming are becoming increasingly evident, the agriculture sector must adapt to ensure food security and sustainability. One crucial aspect of this adaptation is the development and implementation of climate-resilient crop varieties. This subchapter explores the importance of breeding resilient plant varieties for thriving in post-global warming agricultural lands.

Climate change brings about a multitude of challenges for farmers, including increased temperatures, altered rainfall patterns, and the emergence of new pests and diseases. These factors can have detrimental effects on crop yields and quality, posing a significant threat to global food production. However, by breeding crop varieties that are adapted to these changing conditions, we can mitigate these risks and ensure a stable and productive agriculture sector.

Breeding climate-resilient crop varieties involves selecting and developing plants that possess traits such as drought tolerance, heat resistance, disease resistance, and the ability to thrive in poor soil conditions. This can be achieved through traditional breeding methods, as well as advanced techniques such as genetic engineering and gene editing. By incorporating these desirable traits, we can enhance the resilience of crops and enable them to withstand the challenges posed by global warming.

The benefits of breeding climate-resilient crop varieties are manifold. Firstly, it reduces farmers' dependency on external inputs such as pesticides and fertilizers, as these plants have built-in resistance to pests and diseases. This not only reduces production costs but also minimizes the environmental impact of agriculture. Furthermore, resilient crop varieties can ensure a stable supply of food, even in the face of extreme weather events and changing climatic conditions.

To facilitate the development and adoption of these crop varieties, policymakers and agricultural stakeholders must prioritize research and development in this field. This includes providing funding and resources to breeders and scientists, promoting collaboration between public and private sectors, and establishing supportive policies and regulations.

In conclusion, breeding climate-resilient crop varieties is crucial for adapting to the challenges posed by global warming in the agricultural sector. By investing in research and development and implementing supportive policies, we can ensure a sustainable and productive food system for future generations. It is essential that politicians, diplomats, legislators, educators, journalists, and the public recognize the importance of this issue and work together to promote the adoption of these resilient plant varieties in post-global warming agricultural lands.

Genetic Engineering for Climate Adaptation in Plants

In the face of a changing climate, it is crucial to explore innovative solutions for ensuring food security and sustainable agriculture. One such solution is genetic engineering, which holds immense potential for climate adaptation in plants. By harnessing the power of genetic manipulation, scientists can develop resilient plant varieties that can thrive in post-global warming agricultural lands.

Genetic engineering enables scientists to introduce desirable traits into crops, such as drought tolerance, heat resistance, and disease resistance. These traits can help plants withstand the challenges posed by climate change, ensuring stable yields even in adverse conditions. Through precise gene editing techniques, scientists can enhance the natural resilience of plants, reducing their vulnerability to temperature fluctuations, water scarcity, and pests.

One of the most promising applications of genetic engineering for climate adaptation is the development of drought-tolerant crops. As water scarcity becomes a pressing concern, crops that can efficiently utilize limited water resources will be crucial for ensuring food production. Genetic engineering can enable the modification of plant genes to enhance their ability to conserve water, enabling them to withstand prolonged periods of drought.

Similarly, genetic engineering can also help develop heat-resistant crops that can thrive in increasingly warmer climates. By identifying and manipulating the genes responsible for heat tolerance, scientists can create plant varieties that can withstand high temperatures without compromising their productivity. This can be particularly beneficial for regions experiencing heatwaves and prolonged periods of extreme heat.

Furthermore, genetic engineering can aid in the development of disease-resistant crops. As climate change alters the distribution of pests and pathogens, plants face new challenges in defending themselves against these threats. By introducing genes that confer resistance to specific diseases or pests, scientists can create crops that are better equipped to withstand these challenges, reducing the need for chemical pesticides and ensuring sustainable farming practices.

However, it is important to note that genetic engineering is a controversial topic, with concerns surrounding its potential environmental and health impacts. Therefore, policymakers, educators, journalists, and the public must engage in informed discussions and debates to ensure that the development and implementation of genetically engineered crops are done responsibly and ethically.

In conclusion, genetic engineering holds significant promise for climate adaptation in plants. By harnessing the power of genetic manipulation, scientists can develop crops that are resilient to the challenges posed by a changing climate. However, it is crucial to approach genetic engineering with caution, ensuring that its potential benefits are balanced with ethical considerations and rigorous safety assessments. By embracing innovation and engaging in robust dialogue, we can harness the potential of genetic engineering to create a sustainable and resilient future for agriculture in a post-global warming world.

Utilizing Native and Wild Plant Species for Resilience

In a world experiencing the effects of global warming, the future of agriculture is at stake. As politicians, diplomats, legislators, educators, journalists, and the public, it is our responsibility to explore innovative solutions to ensure the resilience of our agricultural lands. One promising avenue is the utilization of native and wild plant species in our farming practices.

Agricultural lands post-global warming face numerous challenges, from extreme weather events to changing soil conditions. To combat these challenges, sustainable farming methods must be adopted. By incorporating native and wild plant species into our farming systems, we can increase biodiversity, enhance ecosystem services, and improve soil health. Native plants are adapted to local conditions, making them more resilient to the impacts of climate change.

Crop diversification strategies are crucial for adapting to post-global warming conditions. By incorporating a variety of native and wild plant species, farmers can reduce their reliance on a single crop and mitigate the risks associated with changing climate patterns. Diverse plantings also promote beneficial insect populations, which aid in pest control and pollination.

Resilient plant varieties are essential for thriving in post-global warming agricultural lands. Native and wild plant species have evolved to withstand various environmental stressors, making them ideal candidates for adaptation. By incorporating these plants into our agricultural systems, we can increase the resilience of our crops and decrease our dependence on synthetic inputs.

Water management techniques are vital for irrigation in post-global warming agricultural lands. Native and wild plant species typically have lower water requirements than conventional crops, making them more suitable for water-limited environments. Utilizing these species can help farmers optimize water usage and reduce the strain on water resources.

Soil restoration methods must be employed to maintain fertility in post-global warming agricultural lands. Native and wild plant species have deep root systems that improve soil structure, increase organic matter, and enhance nutrient cycling. By incorporating these plants into crop rotations or using them as cover crops, farmers can rejuvenate their soils and improve long-term productivity.

Pest and disease control strategies must also be adapted for post-global warming conditions. Native and wild plant species often have built-in resistance to local pests and diseases, reducing the need for chemical interventions. By incorporating these plants into our farming systems, we can reduce pesticide usage, protect beneficial insect populations, and promote a more balanced ecosystem.

Agroforestry practices offer additional climate adaptation strategies. By integrating trees with agricultural crops, farmers can create microclimates, provide shade, and improve water retention. Native and wild plant species can be incorporated into agroforestry systems, enhancing their resilience and contributing to overall farm productivity.

Livestock management techniques must also be adapted to ensure sustainable farming in post-global warming agricultural lands. Native and wild plant species can be utilized as forage for livestock, reducing the need for imported feed and improving animal health. By incorporating these plants into grazing systems, farmers can create more resilient and sustainable livestock operations.

Agricultural policy reforms are necessary to support farmers in post-global warming conditions. Policies should incentivize the utilization of native and wild plant species, provide funding for research and development, and promote education and outreach on their benefits. By supporting farmers in adopting these practices, we can create a more resilient and sustainable agricultural sector.

Lastly, climate-smart agricultural technologies should be embraced to optimize productivity in post-global warming lands. Utilizing precision agriculture techniques, such as remote sensing and data analytics, can help farmers make informed decisions and improve resource efficiency. These technologies can be used in conjunction with the utilization of native and wild plant species to maximize the benefits of these practices.

In conclusion, utilizing native and wild plant species in our agricultural systems is a crucial strategy for building resilience in a post-global warming world. By incorporating these plants into our farming practices, we can enhance biodiversity, improve soil health, reduce water usage, promote pest and disease control, and create a more sustainable agriculture sector. It is imperative that politicians, diplomats, legislators, educators, journalists, and the public support and promote the adoption of these practices to ensure the future of agriculture in a changing climate.

Conservation and Seed Banks for Preserving Genetic Diversity

In a rapidly changing world, preserving genetic diversity in our agricultural crops is of paramount importance. The impacts of global warming on agricultural lands are already being felt, and as policymakers, diplomats, legislators, educators, journalists, and the public, it is our responsibility to ensure the long-term sustainability of our food systems. One crucial tool in this endeavor is the establishment and maintenance of seed banks and conservation efforts.

Seed banks are repositories of plant genetic resources that collect, conserve, and distribute seeds of various crop varieties. These banks serve as a safety net for our agricultural heritage, safeguarding the genetic diversity needed to adapt to changing climatic conditions. With global warming altering the environmental conditions, certain crop varieties may become less productive or even go extinct. By preserving a wide range of crop varieties, we can ensure that we have the genetic resources necessary to develop resilient and adaptable crops.

Conservation efforts go hand in hand with seed banks. Protecting and restoring natural habitats and ecosystems is crucial for maintaining biodiversity and the health of our agricultural lands. These efforts can include creating protected areas, implementing sustainable farming practices, and promoting agroforestry. By preserving natural habitats, we support the survival of wild plant species and their genetic diversity, which can be invaluable for future crop breeding programs.

Moreover, educating farmers and the public about the importance of genetic diversity and the role of seed banks is essential. By increasing awareness, we can encourage the adoption of sustainable farming methods and the conservation of traditional crop varieties. This knowledge sharing is vital for building resilience in post-global warming agricultural lands.

In conclusion, the conservation and establishment of seed banks are essential strategies for preserving genetic diversity in our agricultural crops. As policymakers, diplomats, legislators, educators, journalists, and the public, we must recognize the importance of maintaining biodiversity in the face of global warming. By supporting and promoting seed banks and conservation efforts, we can ensure the long-term sustainability and adaptability of our food systems. Let us work together to secure our agricultural future in a post-global warming world.

Chapter 5: Water Management Techniques for Irrigation in Post-Global Warming Agricultural Lands

Water Scarcity Challenges in a Changing Climate

Water scarcity is a pressing issue that has been exacerbated by the changing climate. As temperatures rise and weather patterns become more unpredictable, the availability of water for agricultural purposes is becoming increasingly uncertain. This poses significant challenges for farmers and the future of agriculture in a post-global warming world.

In order to address these challenges, it is crucial for policymakers, educators, journalists, and the public to understand the implications of water scarcity on agricultural lands. By recognizing the winners and losers in this new reality, we can develop targeted strategies to ensure the sustainability of our food production systems.

One of the key strategies for sustainable farming in post-global warming agricultural lands is the adoption of water management techniques for irrigation. Efficient irrigation systems, such as drip irrigation and precision agriculture, can help optimize water usage and minimize wastage. Furthermore, the implementation of water harvesting and storage techniques can ensure a reliable supply of water during times of scarcity.

Another important aspect is the diversification of crops to adapt to post-global warming conditions. By planting a variety of crops that are resilient to water scarcity, farmers can mitigate the risk of crop failure and maintain their livelihoods. Additionally, the use of resilient plant varieties, developed through advanced breeding techniques, can further enhance the adaptability of crops to changing climatic conditions.

In order to maintain the fertility of agricultural lands in a post-global warming world, soil restoration methods must be employed. Practices such as cover cropping, crop rotation, and organic farming can help improve soil health and increase its water-holding capacity. This, in turn, can contribute to more efficient water usage and reduce the need for excessive irrigation.

Furthermore, pest and disease control strategies must be developed to protect crops in these challenging conditions. Integrated pest management techniques, which involve the use of natural predators and the reduction of chemical inputs, can help farmers tackle pests and diseases while minimizing environmental impact.

Addressing water scarcity challenges in a changing climate also requires the implementation of agroforestry practices. By integrating trees into agricultural landscapes, farmers can benefit from their shade, windbreak, and water regulation properties. Agroforestry can contribute to climate adaptation by reducing soil erosion, conserving water, and providing additional income streams through the sustainable production of timber and non-timber forest products.

To support farmers in post-global warming conditions, agricultural policy reforms are necessary. Governments must prioritize the development of policies that incentivize sustainable farming practices, promote water-saving technologies, and provide financial support to farmers who are transitioning to climate-resilient agriculture.

Finally, the adoption of climate-smart agricultural technologies can help optimize productivity in post-global warming lands. Remote sensing, precision agriculture, and the use of data analytics can enable farmers to make informed decisions regarding water usage, crop selection, and resource allocation.

In conclusion, water scarcity challenges in a changing climate pose significant threats to the future of agriculture. By implementing sustainable farming methods, adopting crop diversification strategies, using resilient plant varieties, managing water resources efficiently, restoring soil fertility, controlling pests and diseases, practicing agroforestry, employing livestock management techniques, implementing agricultural policy reforms, and leveraging climate-smart agricultural technologies, we can overcome these challenges and ensure food security in a post-global warming world. Policymakers, diplomats, legislators, educators, journalists, and the public must come together to address these issues and create a sustainable future for agriculture.

Efficient Irrigation Systems for Water Conservation

In a world grappling with the challenges posed by global warming, the future of agriculture lies in the hands of policymakers, diplomats, legislators, educators, journalists, and the public. As agricultural lands face the uncertainties of a changing climate, it is crucial to explore sustainable farming methods that prioritize water conservation. One of the key aspects of this endeavor is the adoption of efficient irrigation systems.

Water management techniques for irrigation in post-global warming agricultural lands are essential for minimizing water wastage and maximizing crop yield. Traditional irrigation methods, such as flood irrigation, often lead to significant water losses due to evaporation, runoff, and leaching. To combat this, advanced irrigation systems like drip irrigation, sprinklers, and precision irrigation offer innovative solutions.

Drip irrigation, for instance, delivers water directly to the plant's roots, reducing evaporation and ensuring optimal water absorption. Sprinklers distribute water through a network of pipes and sprinkler heads, mimicking rainfall patterns. Precision irrigation utilizes sensors and data analysis to deliver the right amount of water at the right time and location, minimizing waste.

Implementing these efficient irrigation systems requires a multi-pronged approach. Policymakers and legislators play a crucial role in creating incentives and regulations that encourage farmers to adopt these technologies. Educators can train farmers on the proper use and maintenance of these systems, while journalists can raise awareness about their benefits.

Furthermore, it is essential to integrate these water management techniques with crop diversification strategies, resilient plant varieties, and soil restoration methods for a holistic approach to sustainable farming in a post-global warming world. By diversifying crops, farmers can adapt to changing climatic conditions and reduce the risk of crop failure. Resilient plant varieties are specifically bred to withstand extreme temperatures, drought, and other climate-related challenges.

To ensure the success of efficient irrigation systems, it is crucial to address pest and disease control strategies. As global warming alters ecosystems, pests and diseases may proliferate, posing a threat to crop productivity. Integrated pest management techniques, such as biological control and crop rotation, can help minimize the use of harmful pesticides.

Water conservation in agriculture is not just limited to crop production but also extends to livestock management. Efficient water use in animal husbandry practices, such as proper watering systems and waste management, can significantly reduce water consumption.

In conclusion, efficient irrigation systems are vital in the face of a post-global warming world. By adopting advanced water management techniques, policymakers, educators, and farmers can contribute to sustainable agriculture. These systems, when integrated with other climate-smart technologies and practices, will not only conserve water but also optimize productivity, promote soil health, and support farmers in adapting to the challenges of a changing climate. It is imperative that all stakeholders work together to ensure a resilient and thriving agricultural sector in the future.

Rainwater Harvesting and Storage Methods

In a rapidly changing world impacted by global warming, the future of agriculture relies on innovative solutions to overcome the challenges posed by climate change. One such solution is rainwater harvesting and storage methods, which can play a crucial role in sustaining agricultural lands in a post-global warming era.

Rainwater harvesting involves collecting and storing rainwater for later use, rather than allowing it to runoff and be wasted. This practice is not only environmentally friendly but also economically sustainable, making it an attractive option for agriculturists, policymakers, educators, and the general public alike.

There are several effective rainwater harvesting and storage methods that can be employed in post-global warming agricultural lands. One popular technique is the use of rain barrels or cisterns, which collect rainwater from rooftops and store it for irrigation purposes. This method is simple, cost-effective, and can be easily implemented on a small scale. Another approach is the construction of ponds or reservoirs that capture and store rainwater, providing a reliable source of water during dry periods.

Additionally, innovative technologies such as rainwater harvesting systems integrated with greenhouses or drip irrigation systems can further optimize water usage in agriculture. These methods ensure that water is efficiently delivered to crops, minimizing wastage and maximizing productivity.

By adopting rainwater harvesting and storage methods, farmers can mitigate the effects of water scarcity in post-global warming agricultural lands. This not only helps in sustaining crop production but also reduces the reliance on groundwater and surface water sources, which are often depleted due to changing weather patterns.

To encourage the widespread adoption of rainwater harvesting, policymakers, diplomats, legislators, educators, journalists, and the public must work together to promote awareness and provide incentives for farmers to invest in these techniques. Governments can introduce subsidies or tax benefits for implementing rainwater harvesting systems, while educational institutions can incorporate this topic into their curriculum to educate future generations about sustainable farming practices.

In conclusion, rainwater harvesting and storage methods hold immense potential for ensuring the resilience and sustainability of agriculture in a post-global warming world. By integrating these practices into agricultural landscapes, we can optimize water usage, reduce reliance on traditional water sources, and create a more climate-resilient agricultural sector. It is imperative that policymakers, educators, journalists, and the public recognize the importance of rainwater harvesting and work towards its widespread adoption for a sustainable and prosperous agricultural future.

Utilizing Drought-Tolerant Crops and Water-Saving Techniques

In a rapidly changing world, it is crucial for policymakers, educators, journalists, and the public to understand the importance of utilizing drought-tolerant crops and water-saving techniques in post-global warming agricultural lands. As the impacts of climate change continue to intensify, traditional farming practices will no longer suffice. It is imperative that we adapt and implement sustainable farming methods to ensure the future of agriculture.

One of the key strategies for adapting to post-global warming conditions is crop diversification. By planting a variety of crops, farmers can reduce their reliance on specific species that may be more vulnerable to drought or other climate-related challenges. Diversification also enhances the resilience of agricultural systems, making them more adaptable to changing environmental conditions.

Another essential factor in sustainable agriculture is the use of resilient plant varieties. By selecting and breeding crops that can thrive in post-global warming conditions, farmers can increase their chances of successful harvests. These resilient plant varieties are specifically developed to withstand drought, extreme temperatures, and other climate-related stresses.

Water management techniques play a crucial role in mitigating the effects of drought and ensuring efficient irrigation in post-global warming agricultural lands. Implementing water-saving technologies such as drip irrigation, rainwater harvesting, and precision agriculture can significantly reduce water usage while maintaining crop productivity. Additionally, adopting conservation practices such as mulching and cover cropping can help retain moisture in the soil, reducing the need for excessive irrigation.

To maintain soil fertility in post-global warming agricultural lands, soil restoration methods are essential. Implementing practices like organic farming, crop rotation, and the use of compost and green manure can enhance soil health, increase water retention capacity, and improve nutrient availability for crops.

Pest and disease control strategies are also crucial in the face of changing climate conditions. With rising temperatures and altered precipitation patterns, pests and diseases may become more prevalent. Integrated pest management techniques, biological control methods, and the use of resistant crop varieties can help reduce the reliance on chemical pesticides and minimize crop losses.

Agroforestry practices, which involve integrating trees and shrubs into agricultural systems, can provide numerous benefits in post-global warming agricultural lands. These practices enhance biodiversity, improve soil quality, conserve water, and provide shade and windbreaks for crops, making them more resilient to climate change.

Livestock management techniques also play a significant role in sustainable farming. By adopting practices such as rotational grazing, improving animal housing conditions, and minimizing the use of antibiotics, farmers can reduce the environmental impact of livestock production and ensure its long-term viability.

To support farmers in post-global warming conditions, agricultural policy reforms are necessary. Governments should prioritize funding and incentives for sustainable farming practices, provide access to climate information and advisory services, and promote research and development of climate-smart agricultural technologies.

In conclusion, utilizing drought-tolerant crops and water-saving techniques is crucial in post-global warming agricultural lands. By implementing sustainable farming methods, diversifying crops, using resilient plant varieties, managing water efficiently, restoring soil health, controlling pests and diseases, adopting agroforestry practices, managing livestock sustainably, and enacting agricultural policy reforms, we can ensure the future of agriculture in a changing climate. It is vital that politicians, diplomats, legislators, educators, journalists, and the public come together to support these strategies and promote climate-smart agricultural technologies for optimizing productivity in post-global warming lands.

Chapter 6: Soil Restoration Methods for Maintaining Fertility in Post-Global Warming Agricultural Lands

Importance of Soil Health in Sustainable Agriculture

Introduction:

In the face of global warming and its impact on agricultural lands, it is crucial to understand the importance of soil health in sustainable agriculture. Soil, being the foundation of all agricultural activities, plays a vital role in ensuring food security, maintaining biodiversity, and mitigating climate change. This subchapter aims to shed light on the significance of soil health and its preservation in the context of post-global warming agricultural lands.

Soil Health and Sustainable Agriculture:

Sustainable agriculture is centered around the concept of maintaining soil health to ensure long-term productivity, environmental balance, and economic viability. Healthy soil is characterized by its ability to support plant growth, retain water, recycle nutrients, and host a diverse community of microorganisms. These factors are essential for crop production, carbon sequestration, and maintaining the overall resilience of agricultural systems.

Enhanced Nutrient Cycling:

Soil health directly impacts nutrient cycling, which is vital for plant growth and crop productivity. Healthy soils rich in organic matter can efficiently cycle nutrients, reducing the need for synthetic fertilizers and minimizing nutrient runoff. Implementing sustainable farming practices such as cover cropping, crop rotation, and composting can enhance nutrient cycling, leading to improved soil fertility and reduced environmental pollution.

Water Retention and Conservation:

Soil health plays a significant role in water retention and conservation. Healthy soils with good structure and organic matter content have better water-holding capacity, reducing the risk of drought stress for crops. By adopting water management techniques such as conservation tillage, mulching, and precision irrigation, farmers can optimize water use efficiency, minimize water runoff, and enhance overall resilience to climate change.

Carbon Sequestration and Climate Change Mitigation:

Soil health contributes to climate change mitigation through carbon sequestration. Healthy soils can store significant amounts of carbon dioxide, reducing its concentration in the atmosphere and mitigating global warming. Sustainable farming practices such as agroforestry, conservation tillage, and cover cropping can enhance carbon sequestration, making agriculture a valuable tool in combating climate change.

Conclusion:

In a post-global warming world, maintaining soil health is of utmost importance for sustainable agriculture. It is not only crucial for ensuring food security and economic viability but also for mitigating climate change and protecting the environment. Policymakers, educators, journalists, and the public must recognize the significance of soil health and promote sustainable farming methods that prioritize soil conservation and restoration. By investing in soil restoration methods, implementing agroforestry practices, and supporting farmers with agricultural policy reforms, we can build resilient agricultural systems that thrive in the face of climate change. Furthermore, the adoption of climate-smart agricultural technologies can optimize productivity while minimizing environmental impact. Together, we can secure a future where agriculture and soil health go hand in hand, ensuring a sustainable and resilient food system for generations to come.

Soil Conservation Techniques for Erosion Control

In the face of increasing global warming and its impact on agricultural lands, it is crucial to implement effective soil conservation techniques for erosion control. Erosion, the process of soil being carried away by wind or water, can lead to devastating consequences for farmers and the environment. Thus, it is essential for policymakers, educators, journalists, and the public to understand and promote these techniques to ensure sustainable farming practices in a post-global warming world.

One effective strategy for erosion control is the use of cover crops. By planting cover crops such as legumes or grasses, farmers can protect the soil from erosion, reduce weed growth, and improve overall soil health. These crops act as a protective layer, preventing rainwater from directly hitting the soil surface and carrying it away. Additionally, cover crops help in retaining moisture, reducing the need for excessive irrigation, and promoting nutrient cycling.

Another technique that can be employed is contour plowing. By plowing along the contours of the land, farmers create ridges that act as barriers, preventing water from flowing downhill and carrying away the topsoil. This method effectively slows down the speed of water runoff, allowing it to infiltrate into the soil and minimizing erosion.

Terracing is also an effective soil conservation technique. By constructing terraces on sloping lands, farmers create flat surfaces that help to slow down water runoff and prevent soil erosion. This technique is particularly useful in areas with steep slopes, where erosion is more likely to occur.

Implementing soil conservation practices such as no-till farming and strip cropping can further enhance erosion control efforts. No-till farming involves leaving the soil undisturbed by reducing or eliminating plowing, which helps to preserve soil structure and prevent erosion. Strip cropping, on the other hand, involves alternating rows of different crops or cover crops, which helps to break up the flow of water and reduce erosion.

To ensure the success of these soil conservation techniques, it is important to provide education and support to farmers. Policymakers and educators can play a crucial role in promoting sustainable farming practices through training programs, financial incentives, and policy reforms. By prioritizing soil conservation and erosion control, we can create resilient agricultural lands that can thrive in a post-global warming world.

Composting and Organic Amendments for Soil Fertility

In the face of a rapidly changing climate, it is crucial for policymakers, educators, journalists, and the general public to understand the importance of sustainable farming practices in post-global warming agricultural lands. One key aspect of sustainable agriculture is the use of composting and organic amendments to maintain soil fertility. By incorporating these practices into farming systems, we can ensure the long-term health and productivity of our soils while mitigating the effects of climate change.

Composting is the process of recycling organic waste materials, such as crop residues, animal manure, and food scraps, into a nutrient-rich soil amendment. This natural process not only diverts waste from landfills but also provides a valuable resource for enhancing soil fertility.

Compost improves soil structure, increases water-holding capacity, and enhances nutrient availability for plants. By adding compost to agricultural lands, farmers can reduce their reliance on synthetic fertilizers, thereby minimizing the negative environmental impacts associated with their production and use.

Organic amendments, including compost, are particularly important in post-global warming agricultural lands. As temperatures rise and rainfall patterns become more erratic, soils are under increased stress. Organic matter plays a crucial role in improving soil resilience and water retention, which are essential for crop production in these challenging conditions. Additionally, organic amendments promote biodiversity in the soil, supporting beneficial microorganisms that contribute to nutrient cycling and disease suppression.

To encourage the widespread adoption of composting and organic amendments, policymakers and legislators need to support initiatives that promote composting infrastructure, provide financial incentives, and educate farmers on best practices. Furthermore, educators should include composting and organic farming techniques in agricultural curricula, ensuring that future generations of farmers are equipped with the knowledge and skills to implement sustainable practices.

Journalists also play a vital role in informing the public about the benefits of composting and organic amendments. By highlighting success stories and innovative approaches, journalists can inspire individuals and communities to embrace these practices in their own gardens and farms.

In conclusion, composting and organic amendments are essential tools for maintaining soil fertility in post-global warming agricultural lands. By incorporating these practices into farming systems, we can enhance soil health, reduce reliance on synthetic fertilizers, and promote sustainable agriculture. It is the responsibility of politicians, diplomats, legislators, educators, journalists, and the public to support and advocate for the widespread adoption of composting and organic farming practices to ensure a resilient and productive agricultural future.

Soil Remediation for Contaminated Agricultural Lands

In a world that is grappling with the effects of global warming, the future of agriculture hangs in the balance. As politicians, diplomats, legislators, educators, journalists, and the public, it is crucial that we understand the challenges faced by agricultural lands in a post-global warming era, and explore sustainable solutions to mitigate the damage caused by contamination.

One of the key issues that arises in this context is soil contamination. As temperatures rise and extreme weather events become more frequent, agricultural lands are increasingly vulnerable to pollution and degradation. Toxic chemicals, heavy metals, and pollutants seep into the soil, endangering not only the crops but also the health of consumers. This calls for urgent action to remediate and restore the fertility of contaminated agricultural lands.

Soil restoration methods play a vital role in maintaining the productivity and sustainability of agricultural lands. Through various techniques, we can detoxify the soil, remove pollutants, and replenish nutrients necessary for plant growth. These methods include phytoremediation, which utilizes plants to absorb and break down contaminants, and bioremediation, which employs microorganisms to degrade pollutants.

Furthermore, crop diversification strategies can aid in adapting to the challenges posed by a post-global warming world. By growing a variety of crops, farmers can minimize the risk of complete crop failure due to changing climatic conditions. Different plants have different tolerances to temperature, water availability, and pests, ensuring a more resilient agricultural system.

In addition, resilient plant varieties specifically bred to thrive in post-global warming conditions can be a game-changer. Through advanced breeding techniques, scientists can develop crops that are resistant to drought, heat, and pests, ensuring food security in the face of a changing climate.

To support these initiatives, water management techniques for irrigation must be implemented. Efficient water usage and conservation methods can help meet the demands of crops while minimizing water wastage. Proper irrigation techniques can also prevent soil erosion and salinization, preserving the fertility of agricultural lands.

However, it is not just the responsibility of farmers to adopt sustainable practices. Agricultural policy reforms are necessary to support farmers in a post-global warming world. Governments can provide incentives, subsidies, and technical assistance to encourage the adoption of climate-smart agricultural technologies and practices. By investing in research and development, policymakers can facilitate the transition to a more sustainable and resilient agricultural sector.

In conclusion, soil remediation is a critical component of maintaining the fertility and productivity of contaminated agricultural lands in a post-global warming world. Through the implementation of sustainable farming methods, crop diversification strategies, resilient plant varieties, water management techniques, and agricultural policy reforms, we can ensure a future where agriculture thrives despite the challenges posed by climate change. It is imperative that politicians, diplomats, legislators, educators, journalists, and the public come together to support these efforts and pave the way for a sustainable and resilient agricultural sector.

Chapter 7: Pest and Disease Control Strategies for Crops in Post-Global Warming Agricultural Lands

Climate Change Impact on Pest and Disease Dynamics

Introduction:

Climate change is a global phenomenon that has far-reaching consequences for various sectors, including agriculture. As the Earth's climate continues to warm, it is essential to understand the implications of these changes on pest and disease dynamics in agricultural lands. This subchapter explores the impact of climate change on pests and diseases and provides insights into strategies for managing these challenges in a post-global warming world.

Climate Change and Pest Dynamics:

Rising temperatures, changing rainfall patterns, and extreme weather events associated with climate change have a profound impact on the population dynamics of pests. Insect pests, such as aphids and beetles, tend to thrive in warmer conditions, leading to increased infestations and crop damage. Similarly, fungal and bacterial diseases are more likely to occur and spread rapidly under favorable climatic conditions.

Adapting to Post-Global Warming Conditions:

To mitigate the negative impacts of climate change on pest and disease dynamics, sustainable farming methods are crucial. Integrated Pest Management (IPM) approaches that combine biological, cultural, and chemical control methods can help farmers effectively manage pests and diseases while minimizing environmental damage. Educating farmers and providing them with the necessary tools and knowledge to implement IPM practices is essential.

Crop Diversification and Resilient Plant Varieties:

Crop diversification is another effective strategy for adapting to post-global warming conditions. By growing a variety of crops, farmers can reduce the risk of pest and disease outbreaks. Additionally, the use of resilient plant varieties that can withstand climate stressors and resist pests and diseases is vital. Plant breeding programs should focus on developing new varieties that are better suited to changing climatic conditions.

Pest and Disease Control Strategies:

In a post-global warming world, it is crucial to develop innovative pest and disease control strategies. This includes the use of biopesticides, biocontrol agents, and precision farming technologies. By employing these strategies, farmers can target specific pests and diseases while minimizing the use of chemical pesticides, which can have adverse effects on the environment and human health.

Conclusion:

Climate change has significant implications for pest and disease dynamics in agricultural lands. To ensure the sustainability and resilience of post-global warming agricultural systems, policymakers, educators, and farmers must work together to implement effective strategies for managing pests and diseases. By adopting sustainable farming practices, diversifying crops, and utilizing resilient plant varieties, we can minimize the negative impacts of climate change on agricultural productivity and ensure food security in a changing world.

Integrated Pest Management Approaches for Resilience

Title: Integrated Pest Management Approaches for Resilience in Post-Global Warming Agricultural Lands

Introduction:

As global warming continues to impact agricultural lands, it is crucial for policymakers, educators, journalists, and the public to understand the importance of integrated pest management (IPM) approaches for building resilience in farming systems. This subchapter explores the significance of implementing IPM strategies in post-global warming agricultural lands to mitigate pest and disease risks, optimize productivity, and ensure sustainable farming practices.

Understanding Integrated Pest Management:

Integrated Pest Management is an innovative and holistic approach that combines various strategies to prevent, monitor, and control pests and diseases. This method emphasizes the use of biological, cultural, and chemical tools in a balanced and environmentally friendly manner.

Benefits of IPM for Post-Global Warming Agricultural Lands:

In the face of changing climatic conditions, IPM offers several advantages. By reducing reliance on chemical pesticides, it mitigates the risk of environmental contamination and promotes biodiversity conservation. Additionally, IPM strategies enhance crop resilience, reduce production costs, and ensure a sustainable food supply in the long term.

Implementing IPM Approaches:

1. Pest Monitoring and Early Detection: Regular monitoring of pests and diseases allows farmers to intervene at the earliest stage, minimizing crop damage and reducing the need for excessive pesticide use.

2. Biological Control: Encouraging natural predators, such as ladybugs or parasitic wasps, can effectively control pests without the need for chemical interventions, promoting a healthier and more balanced ecosystem.

3. Cultural Practices: Crop rotation, intercropping, and maintaining proper plant spacing help disrupt pest life cycles, reduce pest populations, and enhance plant health.

4. Organic Pest Management: Utilizing organic pesticides and biopesticides derived from natural sources provides an effective and environmentally friendly alternative to synthetic chemicals.

5. Education and Awareness: Educating farmers, policymakers, and the public about IPM practices is vital for successful implementation. Supporting educational programs and disseminating information through various channels can encourage widespread adoption of IPM strategies.

Conclusion:

Integrated Pest Management approaches offer a proactive and sustainable solution to mitigate pest and disease risks in post-global warming agricultural lands. Policymakers, educators, journalists, and the public must recognize the importance of promoting and implementing IPM strategies to ensure resilient farming systems, optimize productivity, and safeguard the future of agriculture in a changing climate. By adopting these approaches, we can build a more sustainable and resilient agricultural sector that can thrive in a post-global warming world.

Natural Predators and Biological Controls

In the ever-changing landscape of post-global warming agricultural lands, it is crucial to explore sustainable and innovative strategies for pest and disease control. As traditional methods become less effective due to shifting climatic conditions, it is essential to turn to nature itself for solutions. Natural predators and biological controls offer a promising avenue for managing pests and diseases while minimizing the use of harmful chemicals.

Natural predators, such as ladybugs, lacewings, and predatory mites, play a vital role in keeping pest populations in check. These beneficial insects feed on harmful pests, effectively reducing their numbers and preventing outbreaks. By encouraging the presence of these natural predators through habitat conservation and the use of companion plants, farmers can create a balanced ecosystem that promotes pest control.

In addition to natural predators, biological controls offer another effective strategy for managing pests and diseases. Biological controls involve the use of living organisms, such as bacteria, fungi, or viruses, to control pests and diseases. These organisms can be applied directly to the crops or released into the environment, where they target specific pests or diseases, leaving beneficial species unharmed.

The use of natural predators and biological controls not only reduces the reliance on synthetic pesticides but also helps to preserve biodiversity and protect the environment. Unlike chemical pesticides, which can harm non-target species and contaminate water sources, natural predators and biological controls offer a more targeted and sustainable approach.

However, the successful implementation of natural predators and biological controls requires education and support. Policymakers, diplomats, legislators, educators, journalists, and the public must come together to raise awareness about the importance of these strategies and promote their integration into agricultural practices. This can be achieved through educational campaigns, research funding, and the development of policies that incentivize the adoption of natural pest control methods.

Furthermore, collaboration between farmers, researchers, and extension services is crucial for sharing knowledge and best practices. By fostering a culture of innovation and learning, agricultural communities can adapt and thrive in a post-global warming world.

In conclusion, natural predators and biological controls offer a sustainable and effective approach to pest and disease control in post-global warming agricultural lands. By harnessing the power of nature, we can reduce the reliance on harmful chemicals, preserve biodiversity, and ensure the long-term viability of our agricultural systems. It is essential for policymakers, educators, and the public to support and promote the adoption of these strategies for a resilient and thriving future in agriculture.

Early Detection and Monitoring Systems for Timely Intervention

In a rapidly changing world, the agricultural sector is facing unprecedented challenges due to global warming. As temperatures rise and weather patterns become more erratic, it is crucial to develop early detection and monitoring systems for timely intervention. These systems will play a pivotal role in ensuring the sustainability and resilience of agricultural lands in a post-global warming world.

Early detection and monitoring systems involve the use of advanced technologies and data-driven approaches to identify and respond to potential threats in real-time. By promptly detecting changes in weather patterns, soil conditions, pest and disease outbreaks, and other factors, farmers can take proactive measures to mitigate risks and protect their crops.

One key aspect of early detection and monitoring systems is the use of weather and climate monitoring tools. By utilizing weather stations, satellite imagery, and remote sensing technologies, farmers can gather accurate and up-to-date information about temperature, rainfall, humidity, and other climatic factors. This information can help them anticipate weather-related risks, such as droughts or floods, and implement appropriate measures to protect their crops.

In addition to weather monitoring, soil sensors and imaging technologies can provide valuable insights into soil health and fertility. These tools enable farmers to detect nutrient deficiencies, soil erosion, and other soil-related issues. By addressing these problems early on, farmers can take steps to restore soil fertility and prevent long-term damage to their agricultural lands.

Another crucial aspect of early detection and monitoring systems is pest and disease surveillance. By implementing integrated pest management strategies and using remote sensing technologies, farmers can detect the early signs of pest infestations and disease outbreaks. Early intervention, such as the use of biocontrol agents or targeted pesticide applications, can effectively control the spread of pests and diseases, minimizing crop losses.

To ensure the effectiveness of early detection and monitoring systems, it is essential to invest in research and development. Governments, policymakers, and educators should collaborate to promote the adoption of these technologies and provide training and support to farmers. Furthermore, journalists and the public should be informed about the importance of early intervention in agriculture and the potential benefits of these systems.

In conclusion, early detection and monitoring systems are vital for ensuring the sustainability and resilience of agricultural lands in a post-global warming world. By utilizing advanced technologies and data-driven approaches, farmers can proactively identify and respond to potential threats, such as weather extremes, soil degradation, pests, and diseases. Policymakers, diplomats, educators, journalists, and the public must recognize the significance of these systems and support their implementation through agricultural policy reforms and climate-smart agricultural technologies. With early intervention and timely monitoring, agriculture can thrive in a post-global warming world, benefiting farmers and ensuring food security for future generations.

Chapter 8: Agroforestry Practices for Climate Adaptation in Post-Global Warming Agricultural Lands

Agroforestry as a Climate-Smart Farming Approach

In the face of global warming and its impacts on agricultural lands, it is crucial for policymakers, educators, journalists, and the public to explore sustainable farming methods that can adapt to the changing climate. One such approach is agroforestry, which offers a climate-smart solution for post-global warming agricultural lands.

Agroforestry is an integrated land management system that combines trees and crops or livestock on the same piece of land. This practice not only enhances biodiversity but also provides numerous benefits in the face of climate change. By adopting agroforestry, farmers can mitigate the effects of global warming, improve soil fertility, conserve water, and increase their resilience to extreme weather events.

One of the key advantages of agroforestry is its ability to sequester carbon dioxide, a major greenhouse gas responsible for global warming. Trees planted in agroforestry systems capture and store carbon, helping to reduce the concentration of greenhouse gases in the atmosphere. This makes agroforestry a valuable tool in combating climate change and meeting emission reduction targets.

Furthermore, agroforestry systems promote soil restoration and fertility. The presence of trees in these systems enhances nutrient cycling, prevents soil erosion, and improves water infiltration rates. This not only increases the productivity of agricultural lands but also contributes to the overall resilience of the farming system in the face of changing climatic conditions.

In terms of water management, agroforestry practices can help farmers adapt to post-global warming conditions. Trees act as natural windbreaks, reducing evaporation and water loss from the soil. They also facilitate the infiltration of rainwater, replenishing groundwater reserves and reducing the risk of drought. This is particularly important in regions experiencing water scarcity due to climate change.

Additionally, agroforestry provides shade and shelter for livestock, improving their welfare and productivity. By integrating trees with grazing areas, farmers can create healthier and more sustainable livestock management systems. This contributes to the overall sustainability of agricultural lands and ensures the long-term viability of farming communities.

In conclusion, agroforestry represents a climate-smart farming approach for post-global warming agricultural lands. Its ability to sequester carbon, restore soil fertility, conserve water, and support sustainable livestock management makes it a valuable tool for adapting to the challenges posed by climate change. Policymakers, diplomats, legislators, educators, journalists, and the public should support and promote the adoption of agroforestry practices as part of a comprehensive strategy for a sustainable and resilient future in agriculture.

Silvopasture Systems for Livestock and Tree Integration

In the face of a post-global warming world, where agricultural lands are experiencing unprecedented challenges, it is crucial to explore sustainable farming methods that can ensure the resilience and productivity of our food systems. One such method is the integration of livestock and trees in silvopasture systems.

Silvopasture systems combine the benefits of trees, livestock, and forage crops, creating a harmonious and mutually beneficial relationship. By planting trees on grazing lands, we can provide shade to livestock, improve soil fertility, reduce erosion, and mitigate the effects of climate change. This integration not only enhances the productivity of the land but also contributes to the conservation of natural resources.

One key advantage of silvopasture systems is their ability to adapt to post-global warming conditions. As temperatures rise and extreme weather events become more common, the shade provided by trees in silvopasture systems can help mitigate heat stress in livestock, ensuring their health and productivity. Additionally, the trees act as windbreaks, protecting livestock from harsh winds and reducing the risk of cold-related illnesses.

Furthermore, the integration of trees in grazing lands can enhance biodiversity by providing habitats for birds, insects, and other wildlife. This promotes ecological balance and contributes to the overall sustainability of agricultural systems.

Implementing silvopasture systems requires careful planning and management. Farmers and landowners need to select appropriate tree species that are compatible with the livestock and forage crops being raised. They also need to consider factors such as soil type, climate, and local regulations. Proper training and education programs should be provided to farmers to ensure the successful implementation and maintenance of silvopasture systems.

To support the widespread adoption of silvopasture systems, policymakers and legislators must recognize the benefits of this practice and develop agricultural policies that incentivize its implementation. Financial support, technical assistance, and research funding should be made available to farmers who are willing to adopt this sustainable farming method.

In conclusion, silvopasture systems offer a promising solution for sustainable farming in a post-global warming world. By integrating trees, livestock, and forage crops, we can enhance the productivity, resilience, and ecological balance of our agricultural lands. It is imperative that policymakers, diplomats, educators, journalists, and the public come together to promote and support the implementation of silvopasture systems as part of a comprehensive strategy for climate adaptation and sustainable agriculture.

Windbreaks and Shelterbelts for Climate Protection

In the face of a rapidly changing climate, it is imperative that we explore innovative strategies to protect and sustain our agricultural lands. One such strategy is the implementation of windbreaks and shelterbelts, which can play a crucial role in mitigating the impacts of climate change on our farms and ensuring their long-term viability.

Windbreaks, consisting of rows of trees or shrubs planted strategically along the edges of fields, serve as natural barriers against strong winds. They help to reduce wind erosion, prevent soil degradation, and protect crops from wind damage. In a post-global warming world, where extreme weather events such as hurricanes and cyclones are becoming more frequent, windbreaks can act as shields, safeguarding our agricultural lands and reducing the risk of crop loss.

Shelterbelts, on the other hand, are larger-scale plantings that are designed to provide protection from harsh weather conditions. By strategically planting trees and shrubs in specific patterns, shelterbelts can create microclimates that shield crops from excessive heat, cold, or moisture stress. This can be particularly beneficial in areas that are prone to droughts or heatwaves, as shelterbelts can help to maintain moisture levels in the soil and mitigate the effects of extreme temperatures.

Implementing windbreaks and shelterbelts not only provides immediate benefits for farmers, but also has long-term positive impacts on the environment. Trees and shrubs planted in these systems act as carbon sinks, absorbing atmospheric CO_2 and helping to mitigate climate change. Additionally, windbreaks and shelterbelts provide habitats for beneficial insects and birds, contributing to enhanced biodiversity and ecological balance in agricultural landscapes.

To encourage the adoption of windbreaks and shelterbelts, policymakers and agricultural stakeholders must work together to provide support and incentives for farmers. This can include financial assistance for establishing and maintaining these systems, technical guidance and training, and information dissemination about the benefits and best practices of windbreak and shelterbelt implementation.

In conclusion, windbreaks and shelterbelts are powerful tools for climate protection in a post-global warming world. By incorporating these systems into our agricultural landscapes, we can enhance the resilience of our farms, protect our crops from extreme weather events, and contribute to the overall sustainability of our food production systems. It is crucial that policymakers, diplomats, legislators, educators, journalists, and the public recognize the importance of windbreaks and shelterbelts and support their widespread implementation for the benefit of present and future generations.

Multifunctional Landscapes for Ecosystem Services and Resilience

In a rapidly changing world, the future of agriculture relies not only on increasing productivity but also on ensuring the long-term sustainability and resilience of agricultural lands. As we face the challenges of global warming, it becomes crucial to adopt multifunctional landscapes that provide multiple ecosystem services while promoting climate adaptation and mitigation strategies.

Multifunctional landscapes are designed to deliver a wide range of benefits, including food production, water management, soil conservation, biodiversity conservation, and carbon sequestration. By integrating different land uses and management practices, these landscapes offer a holistic approach to agriculture that can withstand the impacts of climate change and ensure the well-being of both farmers and the environment.

One key aspect of multifunctional landscapes is sustainable farming methods. Traditional agricultural practices that rely heavily on synthetic inputs and intensive monocultures are not suitable for post-global warming conditions. Instead, farmers need to adopt sustainable techniques such as organic farming, agroecology, and regenerative agriculture. These methods promote soil health, reduce chemical inputs, and enhance biodiversity, thus creating resilient agricultural systems that can adapt to changing climate conditions.

Crop diversification is another essential strategy for adapting to post-global warming conditions. By growing a variety of crops, farmers can reduce the risk of crop failure due to extreme weather events. Diversification also enhances ecosystem services by providing habitat for beneficial insects and increasing soil fertility through crop rotation.

To thrive in post-global warming agricultural lands, farmers need access to resilient plant varieties that can withstand heat, drought, and pests. Breeding programs should prioritize the development of climate-resilient crop varieties that are not only productive but also tolerant of the new environmental conditions.

Water management techniques play a critical role in ensuring sustainable agriculture in a changing climate. Efficient irrigation methods, such as drip irrigation and precision agriculture, can help farmers optimize water use and minimize water wastage. Additionally, the implementation of water harvesting and storage systems can provide a buffer against droughts and ensure a reliable water supply for crops.

Soil restoration methods are essential for maintaining fertility in post-global warming agricultural lands. Practices such as cover cropping, conservation tillage, and composting can enhance soil organic matter, improve soil structure, and increase water-holding capacity. These measures not only boost agricultural productivity but also contribute to climate change mitigation by sequestering carbon in the soil.

Pest and disease control strategies need to be adapted to the changing climate conditions. Integrated pest management (IPM) approaches that combine biological, cultural, and chemical control methods can help farmers minimize the use of pesticides while effectively managing pests and diseases.

Agroforestry practices offer a climate-smart solution for adapting to post-global warming conditions. By integrating trees with crops and livestock, farmers can create resilient landscapes that provide multiple benefits, such as shade, windbreaks, erosion control, and carbon sequestration.

Livestock management techniques also need to be sustainable and climate-smart. Practices such as rotational grazing, silvopasture, and feed management can reduce the environmental footprint of livestock production while ensuring animal welfare and enhancing ecosystem services.

Agricultural policy reforms are crucial for supporting farmers in post-global warming conditions. Governments should incentivize and support the adoption of sustainable farming practices through financial incentives, technical assistance, and research and development programs.

Lastly, the utilization of climate-smart agricultural technologies can optimize productivity in post-global warming lands. Technologies such as precision farming, remote sensing, and data analytics can help farmers make informed decisions and improve resource efficiency.

In conclusion, multifunctional landscapes offer a promising approach to agriculture in a post-global warming world. By integrating various land uses and management practices, farmers can create resilient and sustainable agricultural systems that provide multiple ecosystem services. However, the successful implementation of multifunctional landscapes requires strong political support, policy reforms, and investment in research and development. It is crucial for politicians, diplomats, legislators, educators, journalists, and the public to recognize the importance of multifunctional landscapes and work together to ensure a future of agriculture that is both productive and sustainable.

Chapter 9: Livestock Management Techniques for Sustainable Farming in Post-Global Warming Agricultural Lands

Climate-Sensitive Livestock Breeding and Selection

In a rapidly changing world affected by global warming, the agricultural sector is facing unprecedented challenges. As the climate continues to evolve, it is crucial to adapt our farming practices to ensure the sustainability and productivity of livestock production. This subchapter delves into the importance of climate-sensitive livestock breeding and selection and its role in creating a resilient and thriving agricultural system in a post-global warming world.

Livestock breeding and selection have long been crucial for enhancing productivity and improving the quality of livestock. However, in the face of changing climate conditions, it is imperative to prioritize climate sensitivity in breeding programs. By selecting animals that are better adapted to the changing environmental conditions, we can ensure the survival and productivity of livestock in the future.

Climate-sensitive livestock breeding involves identifying and selecting animals with traits that enable them to thrive in a changing climate. These traits may include heat and cold tolerance, resistance to diseases and parasites, efficient water and feed utilization, and adaptability to new forage varieties. By incorporating these traits into breeding programs, we can develop livestock populations that are better equipped to handle the challenges posed by global warming.

Furthermore, climate-sensitive breeding also involves promoting genetic diversity within livestock populations. Genetic diversity ensures that populations have the necessary variation to adapt to changing environmental conditions. By preserving and utilizing diverse genetic resources, we can increase the resilience of livestock populations and reduce the risk of catastrophic losses due to climate change-related stressors.

To support climate-sensitive breeding and selection, policymakers, educators, and the public must recognize its importance. Investments in research and development, as well as capacity building for farmers and breeders, are crucial to drive the adoption of climate-sensitive breeding programs. Governments should also provide incentives and support for farmers to adopt climate-sensitive breeding practices and promote the conservation of indigenous livestock breeds that have demonstrated resilience to local climatic conditions.

In conclusion, climate-sensitive livestock breeding and selection are essential components of a sustainable and resilient agricultural system in a post-global warming world. By prioritizing climate sensitivity in breeding programs and promoting genetic diversity, we can ensure the survival and productivity of livestock in the face of climate change. It is imperative that policymakers, educators, journalists, and the public recognize the importance of climate-sensitive breeding and support the necessary policies and initiatives to drive its adoption. Only by working together can we create a future where livestock farming thrives despite the challenges posed by global warming.

Rangeland Management for Grazing Efficiency and Resilience

In a post-global warming world, the need for efficient and resilient agricultural practices becomes paramount. Rangeland management plays a crucial role in ensuring sustainable livestock production, and it is vital for policymakers, educators, journalists, and the public to understand its significance.

Rangelands are vast expanses of land that are primarily used for grazing livestock. However, these ecosystems are highly vulnerable to the impacts of climate change, such as increased temperatures, prolonged droughts, and changing precipitation patterns. To adapt to these challenges, rangeland management must focus on maximizing grazing efficiency and resilience.

One of the key strategies for grazing efficiency is rotational grazing. This practice involves dividing rangelands into smaller paddocks and systematically moving livestock from one area to another. By allowing rest periods for vegetation regrowth, rotational grazing prevents overgrazing and promotes healthier forage plants. This not only improves grazing efficiency but also enhances the resilience of rangelands by ensuring their long-term productivity.

Additionally, implementing sustainable grazing management practices, such as proper stocking rates and monitoring of grazing intensity, can help maintain the balance between livestock and vegetation. This approach prevents overutilization of forage plants, reduces soil erosion, and enhances biodiversity in rangeland ecosystems.

To further enhance the resilience of rangelands, the integration of agroforestry practices can be beneficial. Planting trees and shrubs in strategic locations can provide shade for livestock, reduce wind erosion, and increase the overall productivity of rangeland areas.

Moreover, the use of modern technologies, such as remote sensing and satellite imagery, can greatly assist in monitoring rangeland conditions. This data-driven approach enables policymakers and land managers to make informed decisions about grazing management, ensuring the sustainability of rangeland ecosystems.

In conclusion, rangeland management for grazing efficiency and resilience is crucial for ensuring sustainable livestock production in a post-global warming world. By implementing rotational grazing, sustainable grazing practices, agroforestry, and utilizing modern technologies, policymakers, educators, journalists, and the public can contribute to the long-term viability of rangelands. It is imperative that agricultural policy reforms support these practices, and that climate-smart agricultural technologies are developed and implemented to optimize productivity in post-global warming lands. Together, we can create a future where rangelands thrive and provide the necessary resources for sustainable livestock farming.

Improved Feed and Nutrition Strategies for Animal Health

In a post-global warming world, the agricultural industry is facing numerous challenges, particularly in the realm of animal health. As the climate changes and extreme weather events become more frequent, it is crucial to develop improved feed and nutrition strategies for livestock to ensure their health and well-being.

One of the key aspects of these strategies is the identification and utilization of sustainable farming methods for post-global warming agricultural lands. By adopting practices such as organic farming, rotational grazing, and regenerative agriculture, farmers can optimize the nutritional value of the feed produced and minimize the negative impact on the environment.

Crop diversification strategies also play a vital role in adapting to post-global warming conditions. By growing a variety of crops, farmers can ensure a steady supply of nutritious feed for their livestock, even in the face of changing climate patterns. Additionally, resilient plant varieties that are specifically bred to thrive in post-global warming agricultural lands should be prioritized, as they can withstand extreme temperatures, droughts, and other adverse conditions.

Water management techniques for irrigation in post-global warming agricultural lands are another crucial aspect of improving feed and nutrition strategies. With water becoming scarcer and more unpredictable, farmers must adopt efficient irrigation methods such as drip irrigation and rainwater harvesting to ensure that their crops receive adequate water for growth. These practices not only conserve water but also contribute to the overall sustainability of the agricultural system.

Soil restoration methods for maintaining fertility in post-global warming agricultural lands are also of paramount importance. By implementing practices like cover cropping, composting, and crop rotation, farmers can replenish essential nutrients in the soil and enhance its overall health. This, in turn, improves the nutritional quality of the feed produced and supports the long-term viability of the agricultural system.

Pest and disease control strategies for crops in post-global warming agricultural lands must also be emphasized. As changing climate conditions create favorable environments for pests and diseases, farmers need to adopt integrated pest management practices that prioritize biological controls and minimize the use of chemical pesticides. This approach not only protects the health of the livestock but also reduces the environmental impact of farming.

Agroforestry practices for climate adaptation in post-global warming agricultural lands can also contribute to improved feed and nutrition strategies. By integrating trees with livestock and crop production, farmers can create diverse and resilient ecosystems that provide a range of benefits, including shade, windbreaks, and fodder for animals.

Livestock management techniques for sustainable farming in post-global warming agricultural lands should focus on promoting animal health and welfare. This involves providing appropriate housing, reducing stress levels, and implementing proper vaccination and disease prevention measures. Additionally, farmers should prioritize the use of locally sourced, organic feed to minimize the carbon footprint associated with livestock production.

To support these efforts, agricultural policy reforms are necessary. Policymakers should prioritize the development and implementation of supportive policies that incentivize sustainable farming practices, provide financial assistance to farmers, and promote research and innovation in the field of animal nutrition and health.

Finally, the integration of climate-smart agricultural technologies can optimize productivity in post-global warming lands. From precision farming techniques to the use of drones for monitoring and data collection, these technological advancements can help farmers make informed decisions, reduce resource waste, and enhance overall efficiency.

In conclusion, improved feed and nutrition strategies for animal health are essential in a post-global warming world. By adopting sustainable farming methods, diversifying crops, utilizing resilient plant varieties, implementing efficient water management techniques, restoring soil fertility, controlling pests and diseases, practicing agroforestry, and prioritizing livestock management techniques, farmers can ensure the health and well-being of their animals while adapting to the challenges posed by climate change. However, to achieve these goals, agricultural policy reforms and the integration of climate-smart technologies are necessary. By working together and prioritizing these strategies, we can build a resilient and sustainable agricultural system for the future.

Manure Management and Biogas Production for Sustainable Agriculture

In a post-global warming world, the future of agriculture depends on sustainable farming methods and innovative practices. One such practice is manure management and biogas production, which offers multiple benefits for farmers and the environment. This subchapter explores the importance of manure management and biogas production in achieving sustainable agriculture.

Manure, a byproduct of livestock farming, is a valuable resource that can be effectively managed to reduce environmental pollution and enhance soil fertility. Traditionally, manure has been disposed of in open pits or left untreated, leading to the release of harmful gases like methane and ammonia into the atmosphere. However, with the adoption of advanced manure management techniques, such as anaerobic digestion, farmers can convert manure into biogas.

Biogas, a renewable energy source, can be used for various purposes, including electricity generation, heating, and cooking. By utilizing biogas as an alternative to fossil fuels, farmers can reduce their dependency on non-renewable resources and lower greenhouse gas emissions. Moreover, the residual material from anaerobic digestion, known as digestate, is an excellent organic fertilizer that can enhance soil health and promote crop productivity.

Implementing manure management and biogas production systems requires supportive agricultural policies and investments in infrastructure. Policymakers, diplomats, and legislators play a crucial role in creating an enabling environment for farmers to adopt sustainable practices. They can provide financial incentives and subsidies to encourage the installation of biogas plants and the development of manure management systems. Furthermore, educators and journalists can raise awareness about the benefits of biogas production, promoting its adoption among farmers and the general public.

It is important to note that manure management and biogas production are not only beneficial for the environment but also for farmers themselves. Biogas plants can generate additional income for farmers through the sale of surplus electricity or by-products. Moreover, the use of digestate as an organic fertilizer reduces the need for chemical fertilizers, resulting in cost savings and improved soil health.

In conclusion, manure management and biogas production are vital components of sustainable agriculture in a post-global warming world. By implementing these practices, farmers can reduce greenhouse gas emissions, enhance soil fertility, and generate renewable energy. However, achieving widespread adoption requires the support of policymakers, educators, journalists, and the public. Together, we can create a sustainable future for agriculture and mitigate the impacts of global warming.

Chapter 10: Agricultural Policy Reforms for Supporting Farmers in Post-Global Warming Conditions

Importance of Policy Reforms in Climate-Resilient Agriculture

In the face of global warming and its impact on agricultural lands, it is crucial for policymakers to enact policy reforms that prioritize climate-resilient agriculture. These reforms will play a significant role in ensuring the sustainability and productivity of agricultural practices in a post-global warming world. This subchapter will delve into the importance of such policy reforms and highlight the benefits they offer to various stakeholders.

For POLITICIANS, DIPLOMATS, and LEGISLATORS, policy reforms in climate-resilient agriculture will serve as a vital tool for mitigating the adverse effects of global warming on food security and rural livelihoods. By implementing supportive policies, governments can promote sustainable farming methods, crop diversification strategies, and resilient plant varieties. These measures will not only enhance adaptation to post-global warming conditions but also foster economic growth and social resilience in agricultural communities.

EDUCATORS and JOURNALISTS will find value in understanding and disseminating information about policy reforms in climate-resilient agriculture. By raising awareness about these reforms, they can help shape public opinion and foster a deeper understanding of the importance of sustainable agricultural practices. In turn, this awareness can drive positive change and encourage widespread adoption of climate-smart technologies and practices.

For THE PUBLIC, policy reforms in climate-resilient agriculture are of utmost significance as they directly impact food availability, affordability, and quality. By supporting these reforms, individuals can contribute to the creation of a more sustainable and resilient food system. This includes supporting initiatives such as soil restoration methods, water management techniques, and pest and disease control strategies that ensure the long-term fertility and productivity of agricultural lands.

The niches of AGRICULTURAL LANDS POST-GLOBAL WARMING: WINNERS AND LOSERS, Sustainable farming methods for post-global warming agricultural lands, and Crop diversification strategies for adapting to post-global warming conditions will benefit greatly from policy reforms. These reforms can provide the necessary framework and incentives for farmers to adopt sustainable practices and diversify their crops, enabling them to adapt to changing climatic conditions and mitigate the risks associated with global warming.

In conclusion, policy reforms in climate-resilient agriculture are essential for securing a sustainable and productive future for agricultural lands in a post-global warming world. By prioritizing these reforms, policymakers can drive positive change, support farmers, and foster resilience in the face of climate change. It is crucial for POLITICIANS, DIPLOMATS, LEGISLATORS, EDUCATORS, JOURNALISTS, and THE PUBLIC to recognize the importance of these reforms and work together towards creating a resilient and sustainable agricultural sector.

Financial Incentives and Subsidies for Climate-Smart Farming

In order to combat the challenges posed by global warming on agricultural lands, it is essential for policymakers and stakeholders to implement innovative strategies and provide adequate support to farmers. One such approach is the provision of financial incentives and subsidies for climate-smart farming practices. These incentives can help farmers adopt sustainable and resilient methods to mitigate the adverse effects of climate change and ensure food security in a post-global warming world.

Financial incentives play a crucial role in encouraging farmers to adopt climate-smart farming techniques. By offering financial rewards, policymakers can motivate farmers to implement sustainable practices such as conservation agriculture, agroforestry, and organic farming. These methods not only reduce greenhouse gas emissions but also improve soil health, optimize water use, and enhance biodiversity. Financial incentives can help farmers invest in the necessary infrastructure, equipment, and training required to implement these practices effectively.

Subsidies for climate-smart farming can also be instrumental in supporting farmers in post-global warming conditions. These subsidies can be targeted towards the adoption of resilient plant varieties that can thrive in changing climatic conditions. By offering financial support for the purchase of drought-tolerant seeds or heat-resistant crops, policymakers can help farmers adapt to the challenges of a warming climate. Additionally, subsidies for water management techniques such as drip irrigation or rainwater harvesting can assist farmers in optimizing water use and reducing dependence on unsustainable practices.

Furthermore, financial incentives and subsidies can be utilized to promote crop diversification strategies. By providing support for the cultivation of a variety of crops, policymakers can help farmers reduce the risks associated with climate change. Diversification allows farmers to adapt to shifting weather patterns, pests, and diseases, ensuring a more stable and secure food supply.

To ensure the success of financial incentives and subsidies for climate-smart farming, policymakers need to collaborate with educators, journalists, and the public to raise awareness about the importance of sustainable agriculture. Education and outreach programs can inform farmers about the available incentives and subsidies, as well as provide them with the knowledge and skills necessary to implement climate-smart practices effectively.

In conclusion, financial incentives and subsidies have a crucial role to play in promoting climate-smart farming practices in a post-global warming world. By providing support for sustainable methods, crop diversification, and water and soil management techniques, policymakers can help farmers adapt to the challenges of a changing climate. It is essential for politicians, diplomats, legislators, educators, journalists, and the public to recognize the importance of these incentives and collaborate to create a sustainable and resilient agricultural sector.

Land-Use Planning and Zoning for Agricultural Adaptation

Land-use planning and zoning play a crucial role in ensuring the successful adaptation of agricultural practices to the challenges posed by a post-global warming world. In this subchapter, we will explore the various strategies and techniques that policymakers, educators, and the public can employ to support sustainable farming methods and optimize productivity in agricultural lands.

Agricultural lands post-global warming can either be winners or losers, depending on the adaptation measures implemented. By adopting sustainable farming methods, farmers can mitigate the adverse effects of global warming and ensure the long-term viability of their operations. These methods include organic farming, regenerative agriculture, and precision farming, which minimize the use of chemical inputs, conserve soil health, and reduce greenhouse gas emissions.

Crop diversification is another key strategy for adapting to post-global warming conditions. By cultivating a variety of crops, farmers can mitigate the risks associated with changing climate patterns, such as droughts, floods, and heatwaves. Diversification also enhances soil fertility, reduces pest and disease pressure, and increases resilience to extreme weather events.

To thrive in post-global warming agricultural lands, farmers must select plant varieties that are resilient to changing climatic conditions. Breeding programs focused on developing heat-tolerant, drought-resistant, and disease-resistant crops can significantly contribute to the long-term sustainability of agriculture.

Water management techniques are essential for irrigation in post-global warming agricultural lands. Efficient irrigation systems, such as drip irrigation and precision irrigation, minimize water wastage and improve water-use efficiency. Additionally, water harvesting and conservation methods, such as rainwater harvesting and watershed management, can help farmers cope with water scarcity.

Soil restoration methods are crucial for maintaining fertility in post-global warming agricultural lands. Practices like cover cropping, crop rotation, and composting enhance soil organic matter, improve soil structure, and increase nutrient availability. These techniques also contribute to carbon sequestration, addressing climate change mitigation.

Pest and disease control strategies are vital for protecting crops in post-global warming conditions. Integrated pest management (IPM) approaches, including biological control methods, crop rotation, and resistant varieties, reduce reliance on chemical pesticides and promote ecological balance.

Agroforestry practices can play a significant role in climate adaptation. By integrating trees with crops and livestock, farmers can enhance biodiversity, conserve soil moisture, sequester carbon, and provide shade and shelter for livestock.

Livestock management techniques in post-global warming agricultural lands should focus on sustainable practices that minimize greenhouse gas emissions, optimize feed efficiency, and ensure animal welfare. These techniques include rotational grazing, improved genetics, and efficient manure management.

Agricultural policy reforms are critical for supporting farmers in post-global warming conditions. Policies that incentivize sustainable practices, provide financial support for adaptation measures, and promote knowledge-sharing among farmers can contribute to the resilience of the agricultural sector.

Finally, climate-smart agricultural technologies, such as precision agriculture tools, remote sensing, and data analytics, can optimize productivity and resource management in post-global warming lands. These technologies enable farmers to make informed decisions, enhance efficiency, and reduce environmental impacts.

In conclusion, land-use planning and zoning are essential for the successful adaptation of agriculture to post-global warming conditions. By adopting sustainable farming methods, diversifying crops, selecting resilient plant varieties, implementing efficient water and soil management techniques, controlling pests and diseases, practicing agroforestry, employing sustainable livestock management, enacting supportive policies, and embracing climate-smart technologies, we can ensure the future viability of agriculture in a rapidly changing world. It is crucial for politicians, diplomats, legislators, educators, journalists, and the public to come together to support these strategies and create a resilient and sustainable agricultural sector for future generations.

Insurance Schemes and Risk Management Strategies

In a rapidly changing world, the agricultural sector faces unprecedented challenges due to the impacts of global warming. As agricultural lands grapple with the effects of climate change, it is essential to develop insurance schemes and risk management strategies to safeguard the future of farming. This subchapter explores the various approaches that can be adopted to mitigate risks and ensure the sustainability of agriculture in a post-global warming world.

Insurance schemes play a vital role in providing financial protection to farmers against climate-related risks. Policymakers and legislators need to promote the development of innovative insurance products that cater specifically to the needs of agricultural lands in a post-global warming era. These insurance schemes should cover a wide range of risks, including extreme weather events, crop failure, and pest outbreaks. By providing compensation for losses, these schemes can encourage farmers to adopt sustainable farming practices and invest in climate adaptation measures.

Risk management strategies are equally crucial in minimizing the vulnerability of agricultural lands to climate change impacts. Educators and journalists play a pivotal role in disseminating information about sustainable farming methods that can withstand the challenges of a post-global warming world. These strategies include adopting sustainable farming practices such as conservation agriculture, organic farming, and regenerative agriculture. By promoting soil health, enhancing water management techniques, and diversifying crops, farmers can build resilience against climate variability.

Crop diversification strategies are essential for adapting to post-global warming conditions. Diplomats and policymakers need to support research and development efforts to identify crop varieties that can thrive in changing climatic conditions. Resilient plant varieties, whether traditional or genetically modified, can withstand drought, floods, and temperature extremes. By diversifying crops, farmers can reduce the risks associated with mono-cropping and ensure food security in the face of climate uncertainty.

Water management techniques are critical for sustainable irrigation in post-global warming agricultural lands. Journalists and educators can raise awareness about efficient irrigation methods, such as drip irrigation and precision farming, that minimize water wastage. Additionally, policymakers should invest in infrastructure development for water storage and distribution, enabling farmers to adapt to changing precipitation patterns.

Soil restoration methods are vital for maintaining fertility in post-global warming agricultural lands. Agricultural researchers and educators must promote practices such as cover cropping, crop rotation, and organic amendments to enhance soil health. These strategies can improve water retention, prevent erosion, and increase nutrient availability, ensuring the long-term productivity of agricultural lands.

Pest and disease control strategies are essential for protecting crops in a post-global warming world. Policymakers and legislators need to support research on integrated pest management and biological control methods. By reducing reliance on chemical pesticides, farmers can mitigate the environmental impacts of agriculture while effectively managing pests and diseases.

Agroforestry practices can contribute to climate adaptation in agricultural lands. Educators and journalists can highlight the benefits of planting trees on farms, such as providing shade, windbreaks, and carbon sequestration. Agroforestry systems also enhance biodiversity, improve soil health, and diversify income sources for farmers.

Livestock management techniques play a crucial role in sustainable farming in a post-global warming world. Policymakers and educators should promote practices that enhance animal welfare, reduce greenhouse gas emissions, and minimize resource use. These techniques include rotational grazing, improved feed management, and manure management systems that capture and utilize methane.

Agricultural policy reforms are necessary to support farmers in a post-global warming era. Diplomats and legislators must collaborate to design policies that incentivize climate-smart agricultural practices. These reforms may include financial incentives, subsidies, and support for research and development in climate adaptation technologies.

Lastly, climate-smart agricultural technologies can optimize productivity in post-global warming lands. Educators and journalists should highlight the potential of technologies like precision farming, remote sensing, and data analytics in enhancing resource efficiency and reducing environmental impacts.

In conclusion, insurance schemes and risk management strategies are essential for safeguarding the future of agriculture in a post-global warming world. By implementing these measures, policymakers, diplomats, legislators, educators, journalists, and the public can support the resilience and sustainability of agricultural lands, ensuring food security for future generations.

Chapter 11: Climate-Smart Agricultural Technologies for Optimizing Productivity in Post-Global Warming Lands

Introduction to Climate-Smart Technologies

The world is facing a critical challenge in the form of global warming, and the agricultural sector is at the forefront of this battle. As the effects of climate change become more pronounced, it is crucial for us to explore sustainable and innovative solutions that can help farmers adapt to the changing conditions and ensure food security for future generations. This subchapter, titled "Introduction to Climate-Smart Technologies," aims to provide an overview of the various technological advancements and practices that can aid in optimizing productivity in post-global warming agricultural lands.

In this section, we will explore the concept of climate-smart technologies and their potential to revolutionize farming practices. Climate-smart technologies refer to innovative tools and techniques that not only mitigate the negative impacts of climate change but also enhance the resilience of agricultural systems. These technologies encompass a wide range of practices, from sustainable farming methods and crop diversification strategies to water management techniques and soil restoration methods.

We will delve into the importance of sustainable farming methods for post-global warming agricultural lands. These methods focus on reducing greenhouse gas emissions, conserving natural resources, and promoting biodiversity. Through the adoption of practices such as organic farming, precision agriculture, and integrated pest management, farmers can minimize their environmental footprint while maximizing yields.

Crop diversification strategies will also be explored as a means of adapting to post-global warming conditions. By cultivating a variety of crops, farmers can reduce the vulnerability of their agricultural systems to climate-related risks such as droughts, floods, and pests. We will discuss the benefits of diversifying crop portfolios and highlight successful case studies from around the world.

Furthermore, we will examine the importance of resilient plant varieties that can thrive in post-global warming agricultural lands. Plant breeding and genetic engineering techniques have made significant advancements in developing crops that are resistant to extreme weather events, diseases, and pests. These resilient plant varieties can withstand the challenges posed by climate change and ensure stable yields.

Water management techniques for irrigation in post-global warming agricultural lands will also be discussed. With the increasing scarcity of water resources, it is essential to optimize irrigation practices and minimize water wastage. We will explore innovative approaches such as drip irrigation, precision irrigation, and rainwater harvesting.

Additionally, we will delve into soil restoration methods that aim to maintain fertility in post-global warming agricultural lands. Soil degradation is a significant concern in the face of climate change, as it can lead to decreased productivity and increased vulnerability to erosion. We will explore techniques such as cover cropping, conservation tillage, and composting that can rejuvenate soil health and enhance its resilience.

Pest and disease control strategies for crops in post-global warming agricultural lands will also be highlighted. As climate change alters the dynamics of pest and disease populations, it is crucial to develop effective control measures. We will discuss integrated pest management approaches that combine biological, cultural, and chemical control methods to minimize the use of synthetic pesticides.

Moreover, we will explore the potential of agroforestry practices for climate adaptation in post-global warming agricultural lands. Agroforestry systems, which involve the integration of trees with crops and livestock, offer multiple benefits such as carbon sequestration, biodiversity conservation, and soil erosion control. We will discuss different agroforestry models and their applicability in various agroecological zones.

Furthermore, livestock management techniques for sustainable farming in post-global warming agricultural lands will be examined. Livestock production is a significant contributor to greenhouse gas emissions, but through improved feeding practices, waste management, and breed selection, farmers can minimize environmental impacts while ensuring the welfare of their animals.

Agricultural policy reforms for supporting farmers in post-global warming conditions will also be discussed. Governments and policymakers play a crucial role in creating an enabling environment for climate-smart agriculture. We will explore policy measures such as financial incentives, extension services, and research funding that can support farmers in adopting climate-smart technologies.

Lastly, we will highlight a range of climate-smart agricultural technologies that can optimize productivity in post-global warming lands. These technologies include precision agriculture tools, remote sensing applications, data analytics, and farm management software. We will showcase real-life examples of how these technologies are being applied in different agricultural systems worldwide.

In conclusion, this subchapter aims to provide an introduction to climate-smart technologies and their potential for transforming agriculture in a post-global warming world. By embracing these innovative practices, we can create a sustainable and resilient food system that can withstand the challenges posed by climate change while ensuring food security for all.

Precision Farming Technologies for Yield Optimization

In a world that is grappling with the effects of global warming, the agricultural sector faces numerous challenges. However, with the advent of precision farming technologies, there is hope for optimizing yields and ensuring sustainable food production in post-global warming agricultural lands.

Precision farming, also known as precision agriculture or smart farming, involves the use of advanced technologies to enhance productivity and efficiency in farming operations. By utilizing data-driven insights, farmers can make informed decisions about crop management, resource allocation, and pest control, among other factors.

One key aspect of precision farming is the use of remote sensing technologies, such as drones and satellites, to monitor crop health and detect potential issues early on. These technologies provide real-time data on plant health, nutrient deficiencies, and water stress, allowing farmers to take immediate action to rectify these problems. This not only minimizes crop losses but also reduces the need for excessive use of fertilizers and pesticides, making farming practices more sustainable.

Another important component of precision farming is the use of precision irrigation systems. These systems employ sensors and automation to deliver the right amount of water to crops at the right time, based on their specific needs. By optimizing water usage, farmers can conserve this precious resource and minimize the impact of water scarcity, which is becoming increasingly common in post-global warming conditions.

Furthermore, precision farming technologies enable farmers to optimize the use of fertilizers and other inputs. By analyzing soil data and crop requirements, farmers can apply fertilizers and other nutrients in a targeted manner, ensuring optimal plant growth and minimizing wastage. This not only reduces costs but also mitigates the environmental impact of excessive fertilizer use.

In addition to crop management, precision farming technologies also offer solutions for livestock management. Sensor-based technologies can monitor animal health, behavior, and nutrition, enabling farmers to provide personalized care and optimize productivity. This includes precision feeding systems, automated milking machines, and remote monitoring of herd health.

To fully harness the potential of precision farming technologies, policymakers, educators, and the public need to be aware of their benefits and support their adoption. This can be achieved through agricultural policy reforms that incentivize the use of these technologies and provide financial support to farmers for their implementation. Additionally, educating farmers about the advantages and proper use of precision farming technologies is essential for their successful integration into post-global warming agricultural practices.

In conclusion, precision farming technologies offer immense potential for yield optimization and sustainable farming in post-global warming agricultural lands. By leveraging data-driven insights and advanced technologies, farmers can make informed decisions, conserve resources, and minimize the environmental impact of their operations. Policymakers, educators, and the public must recognize the importance of these technologies and support their adoption to ensure a resilient and productive agricultural sector in a post-global warming world.

Sensor-Based Monitoring and Decision Support Systems

In the face of a changing climate and the challenges it poses to agriculture, it is crucial to develop innovative solutions that can help farmers adapt and thrive in a post-global warming world. One such solution is the use of sensor-based monitoring and decision support systems. These systems offer valuable insights into crop health, soil conditions, and water management, enabling farmers to make informed decisions and optimize their farming practices.

Sensor-based monitoring systems utilize a network of sensors placed strategically throughout agricultural lands to collect data on various environmental factors. These sensors can measure parameters such as temperature, humidity, soil moisture, and nutrient levels. By continuously monitoring these variables, farmers can gain a real-time understanding of their crops' needs and make timely adjustments to their irrigation, fertilization, and pest control practices.

The data collected by these sensors can be analyzed and visualized through decision support systems. These systems use advanced algorithms and models to interpret the data and provide farmers with actionable insights. For example, if the sensors detect low soil moisture levels, the decision support system can recommend adjusting the irrigation schedule or applying water-saving techniques. Similarly, if the sensors detect the presence of pests or diseases, the system can suggest appropriate control strategies.

The benefits of sensor-based monitoring and decision support systems are manifold. Firstly, they help farmers optimize resource use, leading to improved yields and reduced input costs. By applying water and fertilizers only when necessary, farmers can minimize waste and conserve resources. Secondly, these systems enable farmers to detect and respond to problems in real-time, reducing crop losses and improving overall productivity.

Furthermore, sensor-based monitoring can contribute to sustainable agricultural practices. By continuously monitoring soil conditions, farmers can identify areas that require soil restoration and implement appropriate measures. They can also track the impact of their practices on the environment and make adjustments to minimize negative effects.

To fully realize the potential of sensor-based monitoring and decision support systems, policymakers and educators must play a crucial role. They can support research and development in this field, promote the adoption of these technologies by providing incentives and training, and facilitate knowledge-sharing among farmers and stakeholders.

In conclusion, sensor-based monitoring and decision support systems offer a promising solution for adapting to post-global warming conditions in agriculture. By providing valuable insights into crop health, soil conditions, and water management, these systems empower farmers to make informed decisions and optimize their farming practices. With the support of policymakers, educators, and the public, the widespread adoption of these technologies can contribute to sustainable and climate-resilient agriculture in a post-global warming world.

Robotics and Automation for Enhanced Efficiency

In the rapidly changing landscape of post-global warming agricultural lands, the adoption of robotics and automation has emerged as a key solution for enhancing efficiency and productivity. This subchapter explores the potential of these technologies and their implications for the future of agriculture.

As politicians, diplomats, legislators, educators, journalists, and the public, it is crucial to understand the role of robotics and automation in sustainable farming methods for post-global warming agricultural lands. These technologies offer immense potential for optimizing productivity while minimizing environmental impact. By automating repetitive tasks such as planting, harvesting, and irrigation, farmers can streamline their operations and reduce labor and resource requirements.

Crop diversification strategies are essential for adapting to the changing climate conditions. Robotics and automation can aid in precision planting and monitoring, ensuring that each crop receives the necessary care and attention. This technology can also enable the implementation of resilient plant varieties that can thrive in post-global warming agricultural lands. By leveraging robotics, farmers can monitor and adjust growth conditions in real-time, ensuring the health and productivity of their crops.

Efficient water management techniques are crucial in post-global warming agricultural lands where water scarcity is a pressing issue. Robotics and automation can play a pivotal role in optimizing irrigation systems, ensuring that water is used judiciously and effectively. By precisely monitoring soil moisture levels and adjusting irrigation schedules accordingly, farmers can conserve water and improve overall water-use efficiency.

Soil restoration is another vital aspect of maintaining fertility in post-global warming agricultural lands. Robotics and automation can assist in soil mapping and analysis, providing valuable insights into nutrient deficiencies and soil health. This data can be used to develop targeted soil restoration methods, ensuring optimal conditions for crop growth.

Pest and disease control is a constant challenge for farmers, especially in changing climatic conditions. Robotics and automation offer innovative solutions such as autonomous drones equipped with sensors and cameras to monitor and detect pest and disease outbreaks. This technology enables early intervention and targeted treatment, reducing the need for harmful pesticides and minimizing crop losses.

Furthermore, agroforestry practices and livestock management techniques can be enhanced through robotics and automation. These technologies can enable precision grazing and monitoring, ensuring sustainable land use and animal welfare.

To support farmers in post-global warming conditions, agricultural policy reforms are necessary. Policymakers must incentivize the adoption of robotics and automation technologies through subsidies, research funding, and regulatory frameworks that promote their safe and responsible use.

In conclusion, robotics and automation hold tremendous potential for enhancing efficiency and productivity in post-global warming agricultural lands. By leveraging these technologies, farmers can adapt to changing climate conditions, optimize resource usage, and ensure the sustainability of their operations. It is imperative for policymakers, educators, journalists, and the public to recognize the transformative impact of robotics and automation on the future of agriculture and work towards its widespread adoption.

Conclusion: Shaping the Future of Agriculture in a Post-Global Warming World

In the face of the challenges posed by global warming, it is imperative that we take proactive measures to shape the future of agriculture. Our agricultural lands, farmers, and the entire food production system are at stake. However, there is hope. By implementing sustainable farming methods, diversifying crops, cultivating resilient plant varieties, managing water resources effectively, restoring soil fertility, controlling pests and diseases, practicing agroforestry, adopting livestock management techniques, enacting agricultural policy reforms, and utilizing climate-smart technologies, we can adapt to the changing climate and ensure a thriving agricultural sector in a post-global warming world.

One of the key strategies for success in the future of agriculture is the adoption of sustainable farming methods. These methods prioritize environmental stewardship, focusing on reducing the use of synthetic inputs, conserving natural resources, and promoting biodiversity. By adopting such practices, we can ensure the long-term sustainability of our agricultural lands while mitigating the impact of climate change.

Another crucial aspect of future agriculture is crop diversification. With changing climatic conditions, certain crops may no longer be viable in some regions. By diversifying our crop choices, we can adapt to the new climate realities and reduce the risk of crop failures. This will require research and education to provide farmers with the necessary knowledge and resources to make informed decisions about which crops to grow.

Resilient plant varieties are also essential for thriving in a post-global warming agricultural landscape. Through advanced breeding techniques and genetic engineering, we can develop crops that are more resistant to heat, drought, pests, and diseases. By investing in research and development, we can provide farmers with the tools they need to adapt to changing conditions and ensure food security for future generations.

Water management techniques for irrigation will become increasingly important in a post-global warming world. With changing rainfall patterns and increased water scarcity, efficient water use and conservation will be crucial. Implementing technologies such as drip irrigation, rainwater harvesting, and precision agriculture can help optimize water usage and minimize waste.

Soil restoration methods are essential for maintaining fertility in a post-global warming agricultural landscape. Practices such as cover cropping, crop rotation, and organic farming can help replenish nutrients, improve soil structure, and enhance water retention. By prioritizing soil health, we can ensure long-term productivity and resilience in our agricultural lands.

Managing pests and diseases will also be a critical challenge in a post-global warming world. As the climate changes, new pests and diseases may emerge, posing risks to crops and livestock. Integrated pest management strategies, biocontrol methods, and early detection systems will be crucial for effective pest and disease control.

Agroforestry practices offer a promising solution for climate adaptation in agricultural lands. By integrating trees with crops and livestock, we can enhance biodiversity, improve soil health, increase carbon sequestration, and provide additional sources of income for farmers. Agroforestry systems can also help mitigate the impacts of extreme weather events and provide shade and shelter for livestock.

Livestock management techniques must also adapt to the changing climate. Climate-smart livestock production, including improved feeding practices, breeding for heat tolerance, and efficient waste management, can reduce greenhouse gas emissions, increase productivity, and improve animal welfare.

Supporting farmers through agricultural policy reforms is crucial in a post-global warming world. Governments must provide incentives, subsidies, and access to credit and insurance to help farmers transition to sustainable and climate-resilient practices. Policies should also prioritize research and extension services to ensure that farmers have access to the latest knowledge and technologies.

Lastly, the adoption of climate-smart agricultural technologies will play a significant role in optimizing productivity in a post-global warming world. Technologies such as precision agriculture, remote sensing, data analytics, and automation can help farmers make informed decisions, increase efficiency, reduce resource use, and minimize environmental impacts.

In conclusion, the future of agriculture in a post-global warming world depends on our ability to adapt and innovate. By implementing sustainable farming methods, diversifying crops, cultivating resilient plant varieties, managing water resources effectively, restoring soil fertility, controlling pests and diseases, practicing agroforestry, adopting climate-smart technologies, and enacting supportive policies, we can shape a future where agriculture thrives, farmers prosper, and food security is ensured. It is our collective responsibility as politicians, diplomats, legislators, educators, journalists, and the public to come together and build a resilient and sustainable agricultural sector for generations to come.